TEACHER TALK:

WHAT IT REALLY MEANS

by CHICK MOORMAN AND NANCY MOORMAN / WEBER

Library of Congress Catalog
Card Number: 88-982773

ISBN
0-96160-46-2-X

Orders may be placed by contacting either of the following:

Nancy Moorman / Weber
NANCY SPEAKING ... For & About Kids
P.O. Box 1130
Bay City, MI 48706
517-686-3251

Chick Moorman
Institute of Personal Power
P.O. Box 5985
Saginaw, MI 48603
517-791-3533/517-791-6711 Fax

Cover designs by Elizabeth J. Nagel

to our own children and

to school children everywhere:

all of whom have helped us learn these lessons.

INTRODUCTION

This book is about teachers' talk — the comments, questions, commands, and suggestions that teachers direct at students every day. It explores the way teachers talk to children and exposes the underlying "silent messages" that accompany their spoken words. The fact is that eighty percent of all talking in classrooms is done by teachers. Sometimes that talk is lecture. Other times it involves giving directions, reprimanding, reminding, praising, suggesting, discussing, motivating, or explaining. Regardless of its form, from kindergarten through twelfth grade, teacher talk makes up eighty percent of classroom talk.

Your choice of words and your language selections are critical to the self-esteem, the academic success, and the healthy mental and emotional development of your students. There is an undeniable link between the words you speak and the attitudes and outcomes students create in their lives. By selecting words and phrases *intentionally;* by altering your present language; by adding to or taking away from your common utterances; you can empower your students and enhance their learning.

As you read *Teacher Talk*, you will recognize many typical phrases that teachers speak to students. Some, you will learn, are counterproductive and defeating, while others are supportive of academic and affective goals. You will be invited to explore the hidden meanings behind the words, and in many cases, learn new phraseology that will help you strengthen your communication style.

The phrases used in this book were collected in classrooms throughout the country, in homes, grocery stores, libraries, wherever adults talk to children. Our own home was a rich source, as were the voices of our own memories. Our classrooms and those of our friends were valuable testing grounds for collecting, using, and retesting the ideas found on these pages.

The phrases and supporting rationale contained in *Teacher Talk: What It Really Means* are designed to help you take an in-depth look at how you talk with children. Our intent is not to encourage you to feel guilt or remorse over language you have used in the past, but to provide you with new perspectives on old patterns, along with an array of new choices. Use *Teacher Talk* to become conscious of your language patterns and the effects that your style of speaking has on students. Use this resource to question your talk. Is it creating the results you really desire?

You decide which phrases can enhance *your* teaching and help *you* create the outcomes *you* desire for *your* students. Select phrases to include in or eliminate from your speaking repertoire based on your own attitudes, philosophies and beliefs. Consider new concepts that appeal to you and leave the rest behind. The choice is yours.

We wish to thank several people who enabled us to create this book. Hal Peterson gave hours of his time reading the manuscript and making suggestions. His ideas improved both the style and content of this book. Debbie Dukarski and Valerie Barnes managed, filed and phoned. All three of these people lovingly cared for our youngest children so that our professional and personal lives could function as we created this book.

Sue Dabakey and Peggy Lange expertly typed, proofed and edited this material with incredible patience and expedience. This contributions were invaluable.

We have grown tremendously through writing this book together. Thank you for allowing us to share it with you.

Chick Moorman and Nancy Moorman / Weber

CONTENTS

"Look at Andrew's picture."

Andrew has been drawing with such concentration that he appears to be unaware of the activity around him. This is unusual behavior for Andrew, who seldom completes an assignment and sometimes does not even begin. The teacher wanders over to see what has captured Andrew's attention. She is delighted to see an oak tree, black and gnarled, standing up in a drenching shower. In genuine appreciation, the teacher holds the picture before the class and says, "Boys and girls, look at Andrew's picture!"

Teachers often speak in this manner to show exemplary work, to praise, or to motivate students. Although this style of language is well-intentioned, it undermines creativity and diversity, and may generate humiliation where pride is intended.

Public praise builds conformity. "Look at Robert's tree" will get you several trees that look like Robert's. "Let me show you Debbie's dog" will encourage dogs that match Debbie's. Public praise signals the "right" answer. Many students pick up on this clue and use it to give you what you want. In order to encourage divergent thinking and creativity, it is important to structure praise (see page 82) or add a statement that shows you value differences. We suggest "Andrew, I see three things that make your tree unusual. Class, what can you do to make yours unique?"

Sometimes creativity is not your goal, as with penmanship or appropriate spacing on a page of math problems. Even then, "Look at Patty's letters" or "Let me show you how Missy organized her paper" can be detrimental. Some students feel embarrassed when their work is held up as an example. The shy child, or one who has not developed a strong sense of his own uniqueness, has a difficult time with public praise. These students often resent being used as examples. They are so busy resisting or denying the praise in their own minds, that often it does not sink in.

They react unfavorably to public praise because they picture themselves as failures. Doing outstanding work or putting forth extra effort is not their normal behavior, and falls outside of their comfort zone. Public praise serves to strengthen that discomfort. When you praise these students publicly, you may actually dissuade them from the kind of performance you desire.

Regardless of which special needs your students have, an effective strategy is the use of private praise. Go to them. Give them warm eye contact, a wink, or a pat on the back. Descriptively praise their efforts. "You completed every problem on the page." This style of private acknowledgement builds intimacy and can create the security necessary for a safe learning environment.

In order to get in touch with the emotion this issue generates in some students, picture yourself at the next staff meeting. Pay attention to your internal reaction as the principal walks over to you and examines your plan book. Imagine the feelings generated as she holds it up in front of your colleagues and announces, "You want to see some great organization? Look at Mrs. Andrew's plan book!"

"I like the way Linda is sitting."

Regardless of the teacher-training institution you attended, you were probably exposed to this concept. Teachers are taught to ignore the behaviors they do not want and to give attention to those they do want. The philosophy is "Catch 'em being good." If you do not like the way eight or ten students are sitting, pick out one student whose posture you like and direct attention there. Classrooms all over the country are filled with variations of this theme.

"I like the way Amanda is standing."
"Look at how Carlos walks down the hall.
I'm enjoying his behavior."
"I appreciate how Sabrina is working."

Using this style of message works. Amanda's classmates will alter their posture, Carlos' peers will walk more quietly, and Sabrina's groupmates will copy her style of working. Since this strategy obviously works, you may be surprised that we recommend eliminating it.

The issue here is not "Does this technique work?" but "Does it work and model effective communication skills for students?" We think that it does not.

"I like the way Linda is sitting" is not honest, direct communication. In fact, the message is not even intended for Linda. It is intended for everyone else. Linda is being used to manipulate other students into behaving in a similar way. When you do this, you model indirect communication and manipulation. Neither is justified by the end of having all students sitting appropriately.

If you do not like how some students are sitting, we suggest you publicly announce your concerns to the class, giving clear criteria as to your present desire. "I'm concerned about how some of you are sitting. I'd like to see feet flat on the floor, backs against the chairs, eyes looking at me."

If your real interest is in praising Linda, we suggest you tell her privately. Go to her and say in a quiet voice, "Linda, I appreciate the way you are sitting." Describe what it is you appreciate and tell her why. This style of speaking accomplishes the goal of giving Linda attention for her behavior and demonstrates your commitment to honest and direct communication.

"Check yourself."

"Check yourself" is a quick phrase that is useful and adaptable throughout the grades. It can be used with young children as a reminder about noise. "I'm having difficulty concentrating. Please *check yourself* and hear if you're using your inside voice." As students are learning to form letters, the purpose is to have them compare their efforts against the criteria. *"Check yourself* and see if all your letters touch the lines." When students are seated and awaiting an assembly, this phrase can serve to help them examine their choices of seating positions. *"Check yourself* to see if you're sitting by someone with whom you can sit quietly."

"Check yourself" can be used with older students as a way to remind them of what you expect on specific assignments. "I'll be reading your papers this weekend. Two things I'll be looking for are an attention-getting first sentence and an ending that ties it all together. *Check yourself* on these issues before you hand yours in." "Your science notebook will be given points for these seven items. *Check yourself* to see if your notebook contains them."

Whether working with twelfth-grade chemistry students, junior high special education youngsters, or junior first graders, "Check yourself" builds self-responsibility by communicating to students your belief that it is *their* job to check on themselves.

"What's another answer?"

"Mention *a* way to stop the eroding of topsoil."
"Tell *one* way that goods may be shipped to market."
"What is *your* opinion on why we went to Viet Nam?"
"Thank you for sharing your idea. What's *another* answer?"

Each of these phrases is an alternative to creating right and wrong answers in your classroom. Each acknowledges the child's importance and potential for contributing to the group. Each encourages more expansive, creative, and fluent thinking, and enhances self-esteem. We call the strategy "different right answers."

Allowing for different right answers is the opposite of insisting on "*the*" right answer. Questions that require *one* right answer, such as "Why did Columbus sail to the new country?" or "How many legs are there on a spider?" stifle thinking. Brains shut down when students hear an acceptable possibility. After all, they think, "That's probably *the* answer."

Teachers can engage the whole group in looking for answers by asking, "What is *one* reason Columbus may have come to the new country?" or "How are spiders different from other insects?" Generate possibilities and extend learning by asking, "Who can share *an* opinion of what Columbus would be doing if he were alive today?" or "What is an interesting aspect of spiders to you?" You encourage all students to contribute when you respond to answers with a nurturing nod, a paraphrase of the answer, and the challenge, "Who has a *different* answer?"

Different right answers enhance creativity by encouraging fluency and flexibility of thought. This means that a variety of ideas is offered; more possibilities are considered. Original, unconventional thoughts and ideas, so necessary to innovation, are encouraged and affirmed. Creativity flourishes when children are free from the fear of being wrong.

Students' self-esteem is enhanced when they realize that they are valuable members of the group; their opinions are respected and sought; their ideas valued. Different right answers give them the opportunity to be experts and to share their knowledge. They feel proud and competent as the teacher and classmates learn from them.

Different right answers help students become cooperative problem solvers. They develop the talent of looking for more than one solution, and they learn to look to each other for supportive ideas and alternate points of view. Students learn that different right answers are not necessarily opposites and can enhance one another.

"Different right answers" is *a* strategy to improve student learning. It is *one* way to extend thinking and generate possibilities. It is *an* idea for improving student self-esteem and cooperation. It is *one* way that may work for you.

"Check it out inside."

Teachers teach students where to turn for answers. We show them how to look up answers in the dictionary, consult experts, examine an encyclopedia, or read the newspaper. We equip them with the skills necessary to use a reference library effectively . We teach them to look to a variety of resources for answers, but rarely do we teach them to look inside themselves.

"Check it out inside" is a phrase that helps us to help students look within for answers. Each of us has a wise part within, an intuitive piece that knows what is best for us. Learning how to contact, listen to, and trust that inner authority are necessary skills. They are invaluable when life presents us with problems whose answers are not found in the back of the book.

"Not sure which part to audition for the play?
Check it out inside."

"Unclear how to proceed with your term paper?
Listen to the voice within."

"Wondering who to vote for in the class election?
Check it out inside."

"Should you join your friends for a smoke after school?
Check *in*."

The school years are crucial years for students to develop a healthy sense of competence. This is the feeling of confidence in their own knowledge and abilities to make decisions, which will impact them throughout their schooling and beyond. Children who do not feel competent may experience helplessness and insecurity about their ability to make minor decisions and major life choices. Such people may learn to rely on others and may never develop their own internal set of standards. They may search everywhere for answers and for happiness except inside themselves. Teachers can contribute to a child's sense of security and self-confidence by encouraging autonomy and competence with phrases like "Check it out inside."

"Check it out inside" teaches the student to trust his *own* judgment. It helps him develop as an independent, autonomous individual capable of making personal decisions. Having faith in his own inner authority serves a child well by enabling him to resist the temptation to please others at his own expense, or to compromise himself by conforming to peer pressure. The child who has learned to "check it out inside" has been given "life assurance." He can trust his own judgment regarding drugs, sex, and alcohol, instead of relying on the judgment of his peer group.

"Next time..."

"Next time, I want you to wait until I'm finished."
"Next time, tell her what you want."
"Next time, put your name in the upper right-hand corner
of your paper."

"Next time" is a sentence starter that plants pictures in students' heads of what you expect. It focuses their attention on what you want to have happen. It enables them to visualize the positive outcome rather than the negative behavior you wish to eliminate.

"Next time" is an alternative to "don't." Imagine that we just told you, "Don't think of a blue elephant." What happened? Of course, you thought of a blue elephant. The same phenomenon occurs with students. "Don't run in the hall" puts a picture of running in the halls in students' heads. "Don't poke and push" helps them visualize poking and pushing. Whenever you say "don't" you may actually strengthen the exact behavior you want to eliminate.

The phrase "next time" not only plants a positive picture, it concentrates on teaching. Whatever follows "next time," instructs. It gives students useful information for later.

"Next time, walk around Jimmy's blocks on your way
out to recess."
"Next time, let me know if your committee wants
more time to prepare the report."
"Next time, measure your margins to see if they fall
within the 3/4 inch guidelines."

Are you interested in developing a style of communication that gives students clear instructions as to your expectations? Do you want them to create positive pictures of desired behaviors? Then, next time begin your sentence with "next time."

"Say some more."

Research shows that teachers spend up to eighty percent of class time talking. Of the remaining time, ten percent is divided between moving from place to place, silence, and other non-verbal activities. This means that while one person (the teacher) does eighty percent of the talking, ten percent of the class time is divided among twenty-five to thirty other people (the students).

High school teachers' talk is mostly lecture. Elementary teachers split their talking time between lecture and giving directions. Regardless of the form, when it comes to talk in classrooms, teachers take most of the turns. Since discussion and sharing ideas are crucial to learning, this imbalance is counterproductive. "Say some more" is a phrase that encourages *students* to take more turns.

"Say some more" is a way to signal to the talker that it is still her turn. It tells her that you are interested in more information, that you value her opinion, or that you do not understand yet. "Say some more" encourages the student to continue talking. It helps her to supplement her original thoughts and extend her thinking.

When you invite one student to say more, the others hear it, too. It serves as a door-opener, inviting them into the conversation. It communicates to all students that ideas and opinions are valued and desired.

Two variations of "Say some more" that we recommend are "In which way?" and "How do you mean?" These two questions invite students to expand their thinking by encouraging specificity and elaboration. Students are moved from generalizations to more detailed thought.

"Say some more" can help teachers remind themselves that listening is as important a teaching function as talking. When you encourage students to "Say some more," you will reduce your own temptation to philosophize, and will encourage students to think through their own ideas and learn from each other. "Say some more" will give students a greater percentage of talking time and teachers an opportunity to experience how teaching is more than telling.

"Answer in your mind."

Did you ever notice how a handful of students tend to monopolize classroom discussions, or how a few youngsters develop answers quickly and rush to be first? They want to be first with their hands in the air, first to be called on, first to be recognized and praised. And what about those students who do not often volunteer? What are they thinking? What value do they get from the class discussion? Should you call on them when their hands are not in the air, or should you wait until they signal their readiness? Would you have to wait forever for some students?

If you are one of those teachers who have struggled with the questions above, "Answer in your mind" will help. By asking students to answer in their minds, you give all students time to think, formulate answers for themselves, and respond privately. They are less likely to give up, and turn their attention to something else.

When students are allowed time to create an answer mentally, they are more likely to respond verbally. Teachers create thinking time by slowing down the process of verbal reaction. Once you break the pattern of calling on those who get their hands up quickly, the students who previously decided to tune out are more likely to become involved.

"Answer in your mind" diminishes the value placed on speed of response and encourages in-depth, well thought-out replies. Students who think more slowly or more deeply are supported. Creativity, divergence, and extension of ideas have an opportunity to develop.

"Answer in your mind" shows each student that the teacher respects his or her ability to create a meaningful response, and encourages every student to take a stand by risking an answer. When those who are called on share their answers verbally, all students can compare and contrast their ideas in relation to those of their classmates.

Practice answering in your mind at the next inservice program or university course you attend. Listen as the leader asks questions. Notice if you get enough time to answer in your mind before someone is called on. See if you are more or less likely to share your answer aloud when you have had time to think it through. Decide for yourself how this strategy fits you as a learner.

"Thank you for taking a risk."

Some children decide that it is easier to sit silently than to risk reading aloud. Others choose to stand with the bat on their shoulders, rather than swing away. Some opt for the easy "A" in general science instead of signing up for the more difficult zoology. In each case the issue is risk.

Many students have decided that school is not a safe place in which to take risks. Spelling bees, boardwork and public achievement charts can lead to embarrassment, fear and shame. Punishment, ridicule and forced competition can also produce negative effects in our students. As a result, some students choose not to share answers of which they are unsure. Others balk at picking the difficult science project. Some will not try out for the school play. These students have concluded that the price they pay for taking risks and making mistakes is not worth the rewards should they happen to succeed.

"Thank you for taking a risk" is a statement you can use to encourage risk taking on the part of your students. Use it during discussions when students volunteer answers, when they participate in new activities, or whenever they show a willingness to make an attempt. Here are some variations of "Thank you for taking a risk" that will help you to invite students to participate:

"Who'd be willing to risk this one?"
"I'd like five people who would risk responding to this problem."
"That was some risk you took. Thanks."
"Who feels like being risky today?"
"Let's all risk putting our ideas on paper."

When you use "Thank you for taking a risk" and other language that speaks of students as risk takers, you communicate your values and beliefs. You inform students that mistakes are expected and valued in your classroom. You let them know that their willingness to experiment and grow is appreciated.

Risk *pads* are a device that will support your language patterns and encourage risk taking among students at any grade level. We recently observed a middle school math teacher using them with her eighth graders. After she completed a direct teaching lesson on a new concept, she asked students to get out their risk pads. She put a sample on the board and challenged them with the following words: "Take a risk with this one. Work it on your risk pads. Let's see what we can learn from our risks." This teacher validated student risk taking with her language and her behavior. Through the use of special pads with a special name, she legitimized risking in her classroom.

Throughout the school years and throughout their lives, people must be willing to step out of the safety and security of the familiar in order to make the changes necessary for growth and learning. You can help students increase their willingness to take those steps by choosing language that encourages and validates student efforts, through the use of risk pads, and by modeling your own willingness to risk growth. Even though these ideas may be new for you, put them into practice anyway. Take a risk.

"You're late."

Ten minutes after the bell rings, Chelsea turns the knob on the door of her second-hour algebra class and enters. She knows that she is late. Her classmates know that she is late, and anyone who saw her pass through the halls knows that she is late. As she settles into her seat, Chelsea's teacher interrupts the lesson to inform her, "You're late."

This teacher has, without realizing it, used an ineffective category of communication called "giving them information they already have." Since Chelsea already knows that she is late, informing her of that accomplishes no useful purpose. Instead, it draws attention to Chelsea, inviting embarrassment and shame, resentment and resistance.

"You're late" is an accusatory response. Rather than welcoming, it serves to punish the student for showing up and is counterproductive to the goal of getting the student to class on time. It is difficult to imagine Chelsea getting excited about algebra now. Her self talk could well include despondent or resentful questions about why she even bothered to come to class at all.

The impact of "You're late" is not confined to Chelsea. Whatever you say to one child, you say to every child. They all hear the real message, "If you come late to this class you will be publicly humiliated."

"You're late" is one of a series of comments that fits into the "giving them information they already have" category. Others include:

"You didn't do your homework."
"You've lost your place."
"Your term paper is late."

Instead of giving students information they already have, provide them with new information. Change "You've lost your place" to "We're on page seventy-two." Do not inform students that their papers are late, give them information on how that affects their grades, or tell them how they can rectify their mistakes. Your immediate reaction to the situation will help to reinforce or extinguish undesirable behaviors. Too much attention, negative or positive, may give students the fuel they need to continue the offense. Instead of announcing, "You're late," offer a genuine smile of welcome and refuse to become a partner to the interruption. Continue teaching. Discuss the problem later.

Students do not need us to tell them that they have not done their homework, are not paying attention, or have lost their places. They *do* need us to help them solve their problems in ways that communicate acceptance, appreciation, and welcome.

"Where were you when I explained this?"

"Do you know where your seat is?"
"Didn't I just explain that?"
"What did I just tell you?"
"Haven't you started yet?"

The inquiries above fall into a category of communication called "questions to which the teacher already knows the answer." They are thinly veiled accusations that require no answer. In fact, if students do answer, they are often accused of insolence! When teachers ask, "Do you know where your seat is?" or "What did I just tell you?" they are indicating displeasure. Usually it smacks of sarcasm and ridicule.

Asking questions to which we already know the answer indicates disrespect for students. Can you imagine asking an adult volunteer, "Mr. Howard, didn't I just explain that?" or "Mrs. Fraser, haven't you started yet?" Our language reveals the respect we extend to others. By eliminating these questions from our communication repertoire, we can model respect for all people regardless of age or status.

When you hear yourself asking questions of this nature, stop. Ask a different question, this time of yourself. Ask, "What is my motivation for asking this question?" Examine your answer. If the purpose of your response is to communicate anger or irritation, drop the question and state your irritation openly. "I'm angry about having to explain this twice," or "I'm irritated that I have to stop this activity to remind you to stay in your seat."

If your intention is to remind students to get in their seats, start their work, or pay more careful attention during explanations, tell them directly. "Bill, please get in your seat so we can begin. Sally, please start your assignment now."

If you really want to know if Janelle has her assignment done, if Kristen has started yet, or where Matthew was when you gave the information, ask. If you already know, then deliver your real message in clear, direct, respectful language.

"Stop that noise and sit down."

There is a game played in schools everywhere. It is played in kindergarten through high school. It can be played by any number of people and usually features students against the teachers. There are no written rules. Since the game is often played unconsciously, participants are usually unaware that they are planning strategies and executing moves. No one acknowledges that the game is in play, though it is played several times each day. We call this game Command/Resist.

You have played Command/Resist frequently. It goes like this. Teachers command; students resist. They resist, because resistance is a typical response to being told what to do. Both adults and students respond with resistance, reluctance, and resentment when confronted with orders and commands. People do not like to be told what to do.

Students are especially willing players of the Command/Resist game. They are given orders so often that they have acquired the habit of automatically resisting any directive from an adult. They are so busy resisting commands, that they often do not even hear the content of the message. When that occurs, teachers get louder and more demanding in order to be taken seriously. Students respond by digging in their heels, and both teacher and students are left feeling helpless and frustrated. If an emergency or some other serious situation arises, *students do not stop playing,* so the teacher has little chance of handling the emergency efficiently.

Put an end to the Command/Resist game by refusing to participate. Instead of telling students what to do, describe the situation at hand and leave the *what to do* part to them. *You* state the situation as you see it and *they* decide what to do.

An alternative to directing students to "Quiet down" is "I'm distracted by the noise." Instead of "Get back in your seat," announce, "I'll begin when you are seated." "I'm on page forty-two and ready to begin" can replace "Open your books and turn to page forty-two."

Avoiding orders and commands decreases defiance. It communicates to students that you think they are intelligent enough to create appropriate responses once they understand the situation. It allows them to make a choice. When you communicate without commands, you invite students to respond appropriately. You lessen the chances that they will react with resistance and perpetuate the no-win game of Command/Resist.

"I don't want to hear any more tattling!"

The kindergarten teacher heard
"Susan threw sand!"
The second grade teacher heard
"Bobby hit me!"
The fourth grade teacher heard
"Joe looked at my paper!"
All of the teachers replied,
"I don't want to hear any more tattling!"

Children tattle. It matters very little whether or not teachers want to hear it. They will. Count on it. Tattling is popular in the preschool and primary grades, and continues through high school. Whatever grade you teach, you will hear tattling. Yet there are some strategies to help keep tattling and the accompanying irritation to a minimum.

The first helpful strategy is to increase your understanding. Tattling is called "prosocial aggression." It is a *natural* stage in the development of the conscience. It is a necessary and desirable, if somewhat unappealing, part of the developmental sequence. Once teachers understand that tattling is normal and inevitable, they will be less likely to resent it and more likely to deal with it effectively.

Sometimes we reinforce tattling because we need to hear about a situation. If Cindy is stuck in a tree or Terry has hurt himself running in the hall, you want to know. Because you respond out of necessity, the tattling is reinforced. At other times you do not need or want the information supplied by tattling. If Bill ran on the way to recess or Julie kept the soccer ball all recess, you do not necessarily want to know. This tattling springs from a desire to get another child in trouble rather than a wish to be helpful.

It is because some tattling is helpful and other expressions of it are not, that children are apt to overuse it. They do not understand that situations differ, and must be encouraged to consider more than one aspect of any circumstance. The positive intentions of gaining recognition from the teacher and having some control pre-empt other considerations. We suggest that you ask the tattling student, "Is this helpful or unhelpful?" This forces her into a decision-making mode and requires that she do a bit of mental work: deciding, discriminating, problem solving. "Is this helpful or unhelpful?" encourages the student to move the focus from fixing blame and getting someone else in trouble to the decision that is required.

Once the student decides whether her tattling is helpful or unhelpful, let her know that you are only interested in helpful information. This encourages a cooperative classroom climate, since students learn the difference between "tattling" and telling. They learn quickly that your interest lies in helping students to support one another.

Another strategy that discourages tattling is to instruct the tattling student to settle the problem with words. Say, "If you don't like it, tell him not to hit you. Say that you don't like fighting." This language technique moves the responsibility for solving the problem from the teacher to the tattling student. It demonstrates your trust and respect in her ability to take care of herself.

Encouraging students to settle problems with words or asking them "Is this helpful or unhelpful?" keeps the teacher from having to pass judgment on something that he has not seen. It is risky to make decisions, fix blame, or discipline children based on the hearsay of other children. The story you hear may or may not resemble what really happened. Everyone's view of reality is greatly influenced by her own needs and desires.

Children will tattle. Until you accept that fact, you may feel impatience and frustration. We suggest that you relax, accept tattling as normal and inevitable, and lean into it. Enjoy it as an opportunity to use your new language skills and move students beyond tattling to a new level of self-responsibility.

"If I were you..."

"If I were you, I'd choose the first book."
"If I were you, I'd ignore him and walk away."
"If I were you, I'd change the ending."

Notice that advice follows statements that begin "If I were you." When you give advice, only two things can happen. Students can take it or leave it. If they leave it by ignoring or rejecting the advice, the advice-giver grows resentful. ("I gave them a great idea and they failed to implement it. I'll be darned if I'll give *them* any more advice.")

If students take your advice and dislike the results, *they* grow resentful. You lose stature in their eyes. Some students actually seek advice to prove that the advice is worthless. They make sure it does not work. It is a way for them to feel superior by proving the teacher wrong.

If advice turns out to be "helpful," students will return to you for more advice in the future. As their faith in your advice increases, their belief in themselves decreases. They learn to turn away from themselves and seek solutions from others.

When we offer instant advice, we deprive students of the experience of wrestling with their own problems. We eliminate time for them to think, to struggle, and to make personal decisions. Often they resent our quick solution to what they perceive as a complex problem. When we quickly solve a dilemma that students perceive to be difficult, they are likely to feel inferior and unempowered.

Most advice is unsolicited. For example, when our son Matt graduated from elementary school, he was informed by his sixth-grade teacher that he could invite two guests to the graduation ceremony and party. Chick was scheduled to work out of town that day and could not attend. Matt's mother appreciated and accepted the invitation, as did Matt's seventeen-year-old sister, Jenny. A few days later, however, Jenny announced that she intended to bring her boyfriend, Don.

Our son now had a problem and was unsure how to solve it. Should he withdraw the invitation to his sister? Should he tell her not to bring her boyfriend? Maybe he should just avoid the issue and show up at the graduation party with too many guests. He took his dilemma to the teacher. Her response was *immediate*. "You'll have to tell your sister not to bring her boyfriend."

Later that night, Matt followed his teacher's advice. He called his sister at college and told her not to bring her boyfriend. His words were predictable, considering the way the situation was handled. "*My teacher said* Don can't come," he told his sister. His language revealed that he did not own the problem *or* the solution.

This young man was about to enter junior high school. His teacher prepared him poorly for that experience by taking away his opportunity to consider conflicting issues, grapple with inconsistencies, and solve problems on his own. He learned "Adults know best. Kids can't trust their own judgment. Somebody else will think for me and will do it better."

Teachers who empower students do not give unsolicited advice. They see their job as that of helping students generate solutions, sort through their thoughts and feelings, and gain confidence through decision making and problem solving. They understand that it is important for students to make some mistakes in judgment. Learning comes from processing those mistakes and experiencing the positive and negative consequences of decisions. We suggest the following guidelines:

1. Postpone instant advice. *Listen.*
2. Encourage youngsters to keep talking. Respond with "Tell me more" or "Keep going."
3. Restate the problem as a question. "You're not sure which book to choose for your report?" "You're unclear what to do when he calls you names?"
4. Use wait time when you restate the problem as a question. Be silent. Give students time to think. Solutions usually follow.

Clearly, adults have a right and an obligation to share their experiences and ideas with youngsters. We have adult wisdom and it is important that we share it in helpful ways. *Ask* if the student would like help generating ideas. If he answers "Yes," preface your suggestions with sentence starters that help the student retain responsibility.

"How would you feel about...?"
"Would you consider...?"
"How would you like...?"

These sentence starters acknowledge that your suggestion may not be the student's right answer. They make it clear that the student is responsible for choosing and implementing a solution.

Monitor your language this week. Notice if you begin sentences with "My advice to you is...," "If I were you..." or "Here's what I would do about that." If you hear these creeping into your language patterns, consider re-reading the material above. How would you feel about creating a plan to eliminate advice to others? Would you consider implementing steps #1-4? If we were you...

"Choose, decide, act, pick."

Use the four special words, *choose, decide, act, and pick,* to help your students see themselves as responsible for their own behavior.

"I noticed you *decided* to be fired up today."
"How come you *picked* your grumpy mood?"
"What response did you *choose* when the
problems got tougher?"
"How did you *decide* to *act* when the assembly
went overtime?"

Many students do not know that they pick their act. They do not realize that they choose their own attitudes and behaviors. They firmly believe someone or something else is responsible for their actions and their language reveals that belief.

"*He* made me do it."
"*She* gave me a 'D'."
"*He* hurt my feelings."
"*It's* frustrating."
"*That* depressed me."
"My *sister* changed my mind."
"*He* swept me off my feet."
"*Math* bores me."

Students use language to blame the teacher, a classmate, or some other external source for their attitude or behavior. "*He* bored me to death, sixth hour," they complain, disowning any responsibility for the creation of their own boredom. "*She* made me do it over," they whine, giving up responsibility for the part they played in creating an inferior product in the first place. "*She* got me going," they respond, in an effort to blame someone else for their outburst of giggling.

Choose, decide, act, and *pick* are words you can purposefully fit into your teacher talk to put responsibility back on the shoulders of your students. "If you *choose* to do it on the side of the paper, you'll be choosing to do it over" is effective in helping students learn that *you* are not responsible for whether or not they do it over. *They* are. "If you choose to do this amount of work, you'll be choosing an 'A' in here. If you choose this amount, you'll be choosing a 'B'," etc. This helps kids learn that you did not give them a "C," they earned it. Other appropriate examples include:

"I see you two are choosing not to sit by each other anymore during reading groups."
"You didn't bring your library book back? That means you've decided not to check one out this week."
"If you choose to turn your paper in on Friday, you get the grade you earned. If you *pick* Monday to turn it in, you *choose* to lower your grade by five points."

Repetitive use of *choose, decide, act,* and *pick* helps students appreciate that they choose. Repetition is a key. They do not understand the first few times. It takes many repetitions before students really figure out that *you are not doing to them, they are choosing for themselves.*

Recently we witnessed the following scene in a sixth-grade classroom. The teacher was sharing with us her experiences of implementing *Teacher Talk* concepts while her students were out for recess. In the middle of our conversation, one of her students came in with a bloody nose. He cleaned himself up in the restroom and then approached the teacher. "Mrs. Whithelm, I just wanted to let you know I'll be going down to the principal's office. I'm not sure when I'll be back. I *chose* to get in a fight on the playground." When the young man left, we applauded the teacher for her efforts in teaching self-responsible language.

We often tell this anecdote in workshops, but some teachers do not understand its significance. "What's the big deal?" they question. "So what if he said, 'I chose'? The kid still got in a fight."

True, the student did choose to *fight.* Clearly, there is more work to be done with this young man. Someone will need to spend time problem solving with him, creating a new plan of action for how he will choose to behave next time and because the student now owns his actions ("I *chose* to get in a fight."), there is a good chance he will learn to control them.

One day we had the opportunity to be present when a third-grade teacher discussed with her students their experience with a substitute teacher.

Teacher:	"I heard that some of *you chose* to break the rules yesterday when I was gone."
Student:	"You know what she did? She cut our 'choice time' in half."
Teacher:	"And how did *you choose* to respond?"
Student:	"Yea, but she said we didn't need that much time."
Teacher:	"So what behavior did *you pick*?"
Student:	"You don't know how mean she was."
Teacher:	"And what did you *decide* to do?"

The teacher in this example has added herself to the growing number of teachers who are using teacher talk to help their students become more self-responsible. You can add yourself to that list by using *choose, decide, act,* and *pick* with your students to help them appreciate that they choose.

"You decide."

Many times throughout the day students ask questions that place the teacher in a decision-making role.

"May I sharpen my pencil now?"
"Will this book qualify for extra credit?"
"Is it okay if I ask Beth to help me?"

These common questions can be answered quickly and efficiently by the teacher with a simple "yes" or "no," or they can create numerous opportunities to empower students. Phrases like "You decide" can effectively place decision-making responsibilities on students. "You decide" frees the teacher from the authoritarian role by encouraging shared control of the classroom and by getting students in touch with their personal power.

Use this phrase only when your internal reaction is "yes." If it is not okay to ask Beth for help, or if it is not a time that you want students sharpening pencils, simply say "no." Since you feel strongly about the issue, this is not a time to let students decide. On the other hand, if your inclination is to say "yes," then this is an appropriate time to use language that leaves the decision to the child. "You decide" creates an opportunity for students to practice being decisional. It gives them the freedom to make a choice. It is one more chance for them to experience their own power and to exercise independence.

Add a condition to "You decide" to help students develop their decision-making ability.

Q. "Can I sharpen my pencils now?"
A. "If you can do it without disturbing the reading group. You decide."

Q. "Will this book qualify for extra credit?"
A. "If it tells about someone you respect and admire. You decide."

When you qualify "You decide," you give students criteria. They must think. They have something concrete on which to base their decisions. You help them develop both their choice-making ability and their thinking skills simultaneously.

Other phrases that work as well as "You decide" follow:

"It's up to you."
"It's your choice."
"You choose."
"You can pick."
"You get to decide."
"You make that decision."
"I'm comfortable with whatever you decide."

Regardless of which of these phrases you choose, the message to students is one of respect. You are telling them "I trust your judgment. You are capable of making many of your own decisions. You know what is best for you."

"Please make a decision."

"Please make a decision to stay with us or to
go to the timeout area."

"Please make a decision to follow the rules or
to choose a different activity."

"Please make a decision to talk quietly or to sit apart."

"Please make a decision" is a strategy designed to put the ball of responsibility in the student's court. It asks a child to examine her behavior and take responsibility for changing it. It presents a choice that puts her in control of a portion of her school life.

Most of the time students will choose the desirable behavior when asked to make a decision. They will choose to stay with the group, follow the rules, or talk quietly with their learning buddies. When they make these choices, it is important that their behaviors meet the criteria for the choice.

If a child makes a decision to talk quietly, but shrieks instead, or if she agrees to follow the rules and then cheats, we recommend that you choose language that describes the behavior and refers to the decision. "I noticed that you didn't go out when the ball hit you. Your behavior shows me you've decided not to participate in the game." "When you talk during reading groups, you tell me you've chosen not to sit by your friend."

When you choose language that focuses on the student's decision, you stay clear of the persecutor role. Both teacher and student more clearly understand that the student is making a decision to choose a consequence, that you are not arbitrarily deciding to punish her. As the year unfolds and your language patterns contain many variations of "I see you've decided not to sit by each other," each student more clearly understands cause and effect. Many come to realize that the *students* control whether or not the consequences are implemented. They loosen their hold on the perception of themselves as victims and learn to see themselves as co-creators of their own circumstances.

One variation of "Please make a decision" allows the student to decide when she is ready to resume the activity. Some examples are:

"When you decide you are ready, you may rejoin the group."

"When you figure out what you'll do differently and put it in writing, you can move your desks back together."

"When you decide to follow the rules, you can ask Bill if he still wants to play the game."

This style of language not only helps the child see that she is responsible for ending the activity, but clarifies her role in resuming it.

You, the teacher, are responsible for the discipline structure within your classroom. Your language can help students realize the choices and controls they have within that structure. As you continue to use this style of communicating, your students will grow to understand that the choices they make impact what happens to them. They will gradually develop the internal controls necessary for independence and self-responsibility, both of which are ultimate goals of discipline.

"Please make a different choice."

The assembly had already begun. Students sat on bleachers as teachers and administrators stood along the sides of the gym. The speaker, standing behind a podium, was well into his "Just Say No to Drugs" message. Then, two students near the front began a conversation. Their actions were distracting to the presenter. He chose to ignore the behavior and continued his message, but the conversation did not stop. It escalated into giggling and harsh whispers. Soon, other students became distracted. Teachers began to send menacing glances in the direction of the culprits. The presenter continued to ignore the disruption, but the disturbance got louder. No one intervened. The speaker realized it was his responsibility to take some action.

What would you do if you were this speaker? What if you were one of the teachers present? How would you handle the situation?

The speaker considered several choices. He could continue without acknowledging the disturbance. He could move away from the podium and place himself in close proximity to the two disruptive students. He could tell them, "Knock it off," or he could end his speech and walk out.

This speaker made a different choice. He paused and walked toward the students. Frowning, he looked at them and very quietly said, "I'm feeling distracted by your behavior. Please make a different choice." He did not scold, reprimand, or hold the students up to public ridicule. In fact, his conversation was low-key and private. Only the students on either side of the culprits were aware of what the speaker said. He let them know how their behavior was affecting him and suggested that they "make a different choice."

By telling these students to make a different choice, the speaker used language that communicated respect. His message informed these students, "I see you as responsible for your own actions. You control your behavior. You choose your responses to life."

He did not order them to "be quiet." He did not threaten, "If you don't straighten up you'll have to leave." He did not even tell them *what* to do. By suggesting that

33

the students make a different choice, the speaker communicated that he trusted that they were intelligent enough to choose an appropriate response. His words left no doubt that he felt they needed to choose differently and he left the decision of how to respond to them. This communicated to the students that their actions affected him. It helped them understand that their behavior has impact.

Practice the phrase "Make a different choice," with your students. When two children are contemplating a fight, tell them, "We don't threaten with our fists here. Make a different choice." "The rule is that we go to the back of the line. Please make a different choice" can be helpful for a child who is cutting in line. When a student is cheating, say "You're choosing to go out of turn. That spoils the game for everyone. Make a different choice." "That loud voice is distracting to me. I want you to make a different choice" is a respectful way to share your discomfort with the noise level.

Often when students are disruptive or behave inappropriately, we attempt to change their behavior by overpowering them with commands and orders. This behavior opposes an attitude of mutual respect and caring, and is more likely to cause students to resist instead of change. "Make a different choice" shares some of the power with students and allows them responsibility for their own behavior. They are then more likely to respond appropriately by making a different choice.

"Thank you for sharing that. It's not a choice."

Students often express desires that do not fit with common classroom practice.

"I don't want to be in that group."
"I don't want to go to gym."
"I'd like to stay in for recess today."

When students express preferences that do not fall within the normal operating procedure of your classroom, a skillful response is needed. We suggest one that helps students feel heard, lets them know that it is okay to express desires, and clearly defines the teacher's boundaries. One we like is "Thank you for sharing that. It's not a choice."

The first half of this statement, "Thank you for sharing that," acknowledges "I understand that you would like things to be different." It tells students that regardless of the situation, they have a right to be heard and their opinion is appreciated.

The second part of this communication sends a different message. "It's not a choice" informs students of your boundaries. It tells them that some things in this classroom are choices, some are not. This is one that is not.

"It's not a choice" helps students appreciate the difference between being understood and getting their own way. Feeling understood is not always synonymous with getting what you want. Students need opportunities to experience that difference so they can improve their communication skills and create less turmoil in their lives. It is one way to encourage them to ask for what they want, delight in what they get, and comfortably work on any discrepancies between the two. A word of caution. "Thank you for sharing that. It's not a choice" is a statement that requires attention to tone and intent. You must *be* thoughtful and sincere, and *sound* thoughtful and sincere. If you sound flippant or sarcastic, students will sense a lack of respect and will behave in kind.

In order to make sure students hear this message the way you intend, be clear in your own mind about why you use it. Know that it is an honest effort on your part to listen and respond. Feel acceptance of the child regardless of the request. Let your tone communicate acceptance and you will empower students, encouraging a higher quality of response, and a more cooperative, relaxed classroom atmosphere.

"Why did you do that?"

"Why did you do that?" can be asked by well-intentioned educators who desire information they can use to solve problems, or it may be asked by educators wanting to fix blame and deliver criticism. That is why we recommend you carefully consider the issue of timing when you are tempted to use this question.

Students have learned from experience that "why" is often a prelude to criticism. When they hear it immediately following a specific behavior, they do not hear "Why did you do that?" They hear "Why did you ever do something so ridiculous, so stupid?"

Students often hear "Why did you do that?" as an attack. When they perceive the question as an attack, they experience anxiety and defensiveness, which do not lead to clear or rational thinking about behavior. "Why did you do that?" is often a demand, a kind of accusation directed at students that takes the focus off the behavior and creates a power struggle between teacher and student. "Answer me!" the teacher may command.

Many times students simply do not know why they did something. When they do not know, they are not able to accurately articulate why they hit or spit or chose anger. Even if they have the capability to figure out *why*, they are probably too afraid or anxious to give us an answer.

There are times when "Why did you do that?" *is* productive. Later in the day, "Why did you do that?" can generate information useful in the search for solutions. Since some time has elapsed between the behavior and the question, there is less of a chance that it will be heard as an attack.

The next time you hear the phrase "Why did you do that?" notice the delivery. Is it a question or an accusation? Is it a search for solutions or a device intended to fix blame? Is it used to help students or to get after them? Does it really matter "why"?

If it does not matter why a student chooses a certain behavior, do not ask about it. If it does seem important, ask later when the tension and emotionality have dissipated.

"Sounds like you have a problem."

Justin concentrated deeply on the schoolwork before him. As he bore down on his work and his pencil, the lead snapped. Without hesitation, he approached the teacher and announced, "My pencil broke." The next move was up to Mr. Richardson, Justin's teacher. He could choose from a variety of responses:

"Borrow one from a friend."
"Here, use one of these."
"You can sharpen it now, if you wish."
"You'll have to wait until later."

Each of these possible responses represents a teacher taking responsibility for a student's problem. Each communicates "I'll take over. I'll solve the problem." Each indicates a lack of respect for the child's ability and willingness to manage a piece of his own school life.

"Sounds like you have a problem," Mr. Richardson told Justin when confronted with the broken pencil. With those words he kept the responsibility for the solution to the problem with Justin, where it belonged. He reminded Justin just who owned the problem, and sent a silent message that he trusted Justin to come up with a reasonable solution. Justin did that. "I guess I'll have to borrow one," he replied, and returned to his seat.

Sometimes, "Sounds like you have a problem" is enough to prompt students into the search for and discovery of a solution. When it is not, follow your message with "I know you can handle it." Again, this tells students that you are seeing them as problem solvers, and that you have confidence in their abilities in this area.

"Sounds like you have a problem" is also useful when kids tattle.

"Bobby called me a name."
"Marcy won't let me have a turn."
"Terry took my pencil."

In each case, the suggested phrase is helpful. Students so often give their power away. They believe that the other child has the problem, so they are powerless to find a solution. Then they have to wait until the other child changes. This view renders them helpless.

Sometimes students attempt to give their power to the teacher. If you rescue them, you take their power and gradually they begin to doubt their capability and adequacy. They will continue to look to you to solve their problems.

When students realize that *they* own the responsibility for solving their own problems, they take the first step towards resolution. They take responsibility for generating and implementing solutions. They claim their own power and learn, with increasing skill, to live responsibly.

"I know you can handle it."

"If you stay after school to make up the work, you'll miss the band rehearsal. Sounds like you have a tough decision to make. I know you can handle it."

"Both you and Jeremy need to use the equipment in order to finish your project this hour? That'll take some thought. I know you can handle it."

"This test seems impossible to you? I know you can handle it."

In each of the above situations the teacher clearly stated the problem, empathized with the student's feelings, and returned the problem to the student with the phrase "I know you can handle it." It is likely that these students felt understood and cared about. They believed they were taken seriously because their teachers showed faith in their abilities to make decisions, follow through, and live with the outcomes.

Creating "I know you can handle it" as a routine form of support and encouragement will remind you not to rescue students, and to allow them to struggle with and solve their own problems. You will support and encourage while allowing skill practice in problem solving. The understanding of "I can handle whatever life sends me" is crucial to mental health and to happiness. One of the leading reasons that adults seek counseling is their perceived inability to manage whatever life sends them. We cannot always control the circumstances in our lives, but we must feel secure that we *can* cope with them. "I know you can handle it" communicates your respect for the students' ability to manage their own lives.

"Every problem has a solution."

Rick has a problem. His science project is due in one week, and he has not started it yet. Bonnie has a problem, too. Her best friend just moved to New Jersey and she feels sad.

How will these students react to their problems? What attitudes, efforts and resources will they choose? Their reactions may depend on how skillfully you demonstrate your beliefs about problems.

Problem solving is made up of skills such as problem identification, brainstorming possible solutions, consensus seeking, weighing alternatives, goal setting, and evaluating. Often students do not possess these skills, so they disown their problems, blame others, lie, or pretend that the problem does not exist. In addition, they often hold erroneous beliefs that hinder effective problem solving. They believe that they do not have the *ability* to be successful problem solvers.

"Every problem has a solution" is a phrase that will help your students begin to see themselves as problem solvers. Use it often. Say it as you debrief with three students who have tussled on the bus. Repeat it as you discuss with students possible ways to reduce the number of incomplete assignments in your senior English class. Vocalize it as you struggle to open a stuck desk drawer in front of the group. As your students are exposed to "Every problem has a solution" throughout the year, they will come to understand that you firmly believe it. Slowly, it will sink into their minds and will be available when they need it.

"Every problem has a solution" must be lived as well as spoken. Students need to see us demonstrate our belief in this philosophy if they are to believe it. If there is a discrepancy between what we say and what we do, students imitate what we do. Our actions, as well as our words, must demonstrate our belief that every problem has a solution. From now on, when problems occur, make the search for solutions more important than fixing blame and handing out punishment. If someone spills paint, see the situation as an opportunity to model effective handling of a problem. Instead of rushing to find out who did it, focus on finding a solution to the immediate problem. Let your students witness how a mature adult approaches and solves the problem of paint on the floor. When the crisis is over and the paint cleaned up, use the incident to model a problem-solving process to students while producing a solution that will prevent more spills. Help students define the problem, list possible solutions, consider the alternatives, and reach consensus on a solution. Involve students in monitoring the implementation of the plan and evaluating the success of the solution.

Students need to actively experience a problem-solving process many times before it becomes internalized. They must have it explained and modeled for them over and over. You must *use* it in your classroom if you want to teach it. Use it for such problems as too much pencil sharpening during reading time, too many tardies after lunch, too many put-downs during lunch hour. Use the process with individuals who continuously show up for class without materials, dominate class discussions, or plagiarize written assignments.

When both your actions and your words communicate "Every problem has a solution," you encourage students to give up helplessness and replace it with confidence in their own skills and abilities. You teach them to interpret the roadblocks of their lives as opportunities to learn and grow. You teach them that instead of complaining and disowning their responsibility for problems, they can face their problems and solve them.

"I want you to help me solve my problem."

Jackie likes to chew gum. Most of her teachers do not care, but her Home Economics teacher, Ms. Weber, does care. In fact, she has already spoken to Jackie about gum chewing three times this week. Now she has asked to speak to Jackie after school.

Bob enjoys math and respects Mr. Hodgekiss, his second-hour teacher, but he often forgets to bring his math book to class. That happened twice last week. Today he showed up without his book again, and Mr. Hodgekiss requested a meeting during lunch hour.

Pedro loves kindergarten, his classmates, and Ms. Barnes. He especially enjoys sitting on the rug while she reads a story and shows the pictures. He likes the stories so much that he often blurts out his opinions when Ms. Barnes pauses for a breath. Today she suggested that they chat during playtime.

These teachers have many things in common. Each has a student choosing a behavior that interferes with the learning process. Each is tired of dealing with the situation and each has arranged for a private meeting. Each teacher will begin the meeting with one of our favorite phrases, "I want you to help me solve my problem."

In each of these cases a one-on-one problem-solving meeting will occur. Students will be confronted with their behavior and invited to help the teacher find a solution. It is important to the success of this approach that the teacher believe that *it is not the students, but the teacher who has the problem.*

If gum chewing bothers Ms. Weber, and one of her students chews gum, then Ms. Weber has the problem. If Ms. Barnes feels irritated by Pedro's outbursts, she has the problem. If Mr. Hodgekiss has to stop lessons to find materials for Bob, it is Mr. Hodgekiss who has the problem.

Some teachers believe that in the above examples, the students have the problem. After all, they reason, the students are the ones chewing gum, coming to class unprepared, or interrupting. The students are breaking the rules. Since *they* are activating the behavior, *they* have the problem. A different point of view, however, is that the gum chewing is not a problem to the student. It only bothers Ms. Weber. The interruptions do not disturb Pedro, only his teacher. While it is certainly true that in each case both the teacher and the student will benefit from a change in behavior, it is really the *teacher* who has the problem.

If teachers enter a problem-solving meeting believing that the student has a problem, they naturally talk and act as if the student is wrong. Even if the words and demeanor are caring and gentle, the student can hardly escape feeling accused. The common reaction is defensiveness and resistance, because when students feel pushed, they push back. Now they are unable to genuinely listen to the problem and help to create a solution. The stance, "*You* have a problem," has failed.

When teachers communicate from the "I want you to help me solve *my* problem" approach, students feel invited and respected. Cooperation and *mutual* problem solving are encouraged. Students are more likely to understand the teacher's problem and less likely to view the teacher as the adversary.

When you invite students to help you solve *your* problem, you encourage them to join you in the search for solutions. You ask them to make a personal investment in the problem, which greatly enhances the chances that the problem solving will result in a workable solution.

All three of the teachers in the previous examples knew that they had problems and invited students to help them solve their problems. Jackie and her teacher agreed that gum would be chewed one day per week only. Jackie could pick the day and the teacher retained veto power. Bob volunteered to take his math book to his first-hour class so he would not have to return to his locker before math. Pedro and his teacher created a special hand signal to remind Pedro that he needed to wait before speaking. Just talking seriously with him in this respectful, caring way focused Pedro's attention on the problem and his behavior changed significantly.

These teachers have a lot in common. Each helped a student participate in a problem-solving process. Each found a mutually acceptable solution with students without feeling the need to "pull-rank." Each modeled effective problem solving and communication skills, and each discovered the value of "I want you to help me solve my problem."

"Hurry up."

"Let's get going."
"Get a move on."
"Come on!"

These are all versions of the phrase "Hurry up." They are characteristic of the "hurry-up sickness" that pervades our educational system.

Time's up. Take it home. Finish it later. Hurry up and get them ready for junior high. Turn kindergarten into mini first grades. The sooner the better. Hurry their progress. Hurry the expectations. The year is just about over. Time is just about up. Let's go!

Why such a premium on going fast? What is the rush? Is speed important? Is it helpful to get students to work faster? Is it educationally sound?

Our belief is that the desire for speed and closure is harmful to students. It works against in-depth exploration of concepts and materials, and creates surface skimmers.

Surface skimmers may be elementary students who wander aimlessly around the room twenty minutes after you put a full morning's assignments on the board. Yvonne is typical. You spot her talking with another student. Gently you remind her to get back to work, but she insists that she is done. After working only twenty minutes on four assignments she thinks she is done? You request to see her work. Guess what? She *is* done. Every assignment is finished. Barely. Yvonne has done nothing in-depth. Her work shows that she has not thought deeply about it, nor invested much of herself in it. Yet, it *is* done. She has effectively skimmed the surface of every assigned task.

Secondary school surface skimmers ask "Will this count towards our grade?" If the assignment is not graded, they are uninterested. Surface skimmers do the minimum requirement, but no more. If you ask for five, they do five. If you require one paragraph, they will do only one. Surface skimming is commonplace and frustrating, and we ask for it. In fact, we actually create surface skimmers by combining two phenomena in our classrooms.

The first phenomenon is that we pay off for getting done quickly. If kids get done, they do not have homework. If they get done, they get to go out for recess. If they get done, they get to help the teacher, have extra minutes of choice time, and get approving comments on their report cards. If they get done, their parents get to hear that they are industrious and cooperative. If students do not get done, they are in trouble. They lose recess, have homework, and miss choice time. They are rushed and are often denied the opportunity to finish what they started.

Students learn early in their school lives that smart kids get done fast and dumb kids take a long time. When our daughter Jenny entered fifth grade, she insisted that this was the best teacher, the best class, ever. She based her evaluation on many criteria, but number one on her list was "This year I'm the third one done." Getting done is so important to children that they all know the getting-done order in their classrooms.

The second phenomenon we combine with paying off for getting done is the type of tasks we arrange. Many of the assignments we ask students to do can be completed in one sitting. Ditto sheets, workbook pages, and end of the chapter questions are all activities that students can get done in one allotted time slot.

It is easy to see why students rush to get done with assignments and why many of them are surface skimmers. First, we create task after task that students can finish in one sitting. Then, we pay off for getting done fast.

If you notice surface skimming and hurry-up sickness in your classroom, create tasks that students cannot complete in one sitting. Design some activities that force them to extend their interest over a period of days or even weeks. Papier-mache is an example of an activity that cannot be completed in one sitting. The student has to work on it, let it dry, work on it, let it dry, over and over again for several days. Then they have to sand it, paint it, touch it up, etc. It simply cannot be done in a single sitting. It is difficult to skim the surface when an activity requires a commitment of several days.

Revising and editing a project over a period of days will help students do more in-depth work and will serve as an antidote to hurry-up sickness. This can be done with even the youngest beginning writers and artists.

Another way to slow the rush to completion is to pay off for in-depth work. Value and reward students who go beyond the minimum. Communicate your acceptance and appreciation of precision and detail, creativity and elaboration.

Another strategy to combat hurry-up sickness is to stagger some activities so that students who have not completed an activity can have the time to do so. Schedule reading to the class right after math seatwork, so that students who work more slowly can enjoy the story while they complete their math assignment. (Yes, most students can do two things at once!)

When you hear yourself suggest to students that they "Hurry up," ask yourself, "Why? Is hurrying to finish only a convenience? Is it in the best educational interests of my students? What do I really want to communicate here?"

Take your time as you formulate your answers. There is no need to hurry up.

"Do you want some help or do you want more time?"

Aaron was a slightly uncomfortable, often disconcerted third grader. He was anxious to learn and anxious to please. In fact, Aaron was anxious much of the time. When a group question was asked, Aaron's hand shot up to offer a reply, but usually no answer was forthcoming. The teacher was confounded. She knew about "wait time" and routinely gave the children ten or twelve seconds to formulate a response. She did not know if Aaron was growing embarrassed with his own silence or if he was a child who simply enjoyed the attention of being called on. Aaron seemed bright, but when he volunteered he seldom actually did answer. Eventually, the teacher would move on. Then, one time the teacher asked him, "Aaron, do you want some help or do you want more time?"

Aaron smiled. "More time," he responded. The teacher was surprised, but as she watched him and waited for what seemed to be an eternity, she recognized that the "wheels were turning." When Aaron spoke, the answer was clear, reasonable, and creative. He beamed and so did the teacher.

The teacher learned through this incident that Aaron required twenty- to twenty-five seconds to process a question and create an answer. When given the time he needed, Aaron could respond satisfactorily. He had continually volunteered because he knew he was up to the question. Imagine if those capabilities had been ignored or if the teacher had assumed Aaron was not intelligent! Imagine if Aaron had tired of the teacher moving on to someone else and had given up. His self-esteem and learning, as well as the learning of the whole class, would have suffered.

Aaron's teacher began to wonder if other students needed more time to process questions and formulate answers. She initiated a process to find out. She instructed the children that following a question they were to wait for a nod from her before they raised their hands. In this way, every student had ample thinking time without the pressure or distraction of other students volunteering. They were not pressured by the teacher or their peers to hurry up their learning. The teacher found that many children had shut down their thinking when the first hand went up. She now noticed more students volunteering *and* responding.

Because of this new process, Aaron and the other third graders learned that being first with an answer was not valued in their class. Thoughtful answers were valued. They learned that when it was their turn, they could take their time. They would be asked "Do you want some help or do you want more time?"

"This is going to be hard."

"Today we'll start a form of long division that is difficult."
"Second grade is hard."
"This vocabulary list is a tough one."

The sentences above are all variations of the same theme. Each is an attempt to impress on students the seriousness of an upcoming activity. Each is delivered as a gentle warning. Each may be more harmful than helpful.

Warnings, though well-intentioned, plant doubt in students' minds. They are negative predictors of things to come and are often the first step in a string of events that lead to a self-fulfilling prophesy.

If first graders are frequently reminded of the difficulties that await them the following year, they will develop negative expectations. They will believe that second grade will be hard. Their perception of second grade may cause them to create second grade as hard, because they will focus on the aspects that match their beliefs. Second grade may indeed be hard for them.

Warnings like "This test will be a tough one" are sometimes delivered so that students will take the test seriously and will study harder. This technique tells students that we believe they are not responsible enough to take exams seriously unless we scare them.

We suggest that you avoid negative predictions. Concentrate instead on giving students the information necessary to make their own determinations about levels of difficulty. Replace words like "hard," "difficult," or "tough" with clear descriptions. Simply give them the facts. "There will be forty questions on this test. Three will be essay. The rest are fill in the blank. All come from information covered in the chapter about early settlers." Instead of warning students about junior high, tell them exactly what is expected of seventh graders. Detail the skills necessary to perform long division without mentioning difficulty.

When you concentrate on giving students information without projecting negative expectations, your words help move them toward your goal of taking the test, the assignment, or the grade seriously.

"There you go again."

"There you go again" is a phrase that can have positive or negative effects. That depends on how you use it. Some teachers use it to point out negative behaviors. "There you go again, getting out of your seat." "Another fight on the playground? Here we go again."

When used to draw students' attention to negative actions, "There you go again" is unhelpful. It communicates your negative expectations and verbally reinforces the behavior you desire to eliminate. It converts the past to the present, branding students as *that way,* and encourages both you and the child to project present behavior into the future.

A special variation of "There you go again" involves keeping score. "That's the third time you've forgotten your homework this week." "That's five! One more time out of your seat this morning will make a half dozen." While mental score keeping may serve the purpose of helping you detect patterns in student behavior, it is not helpful information to share with the child. Announcing your scorekeeping communicates to students that you see their present behavior as part of a series. This implies a prediction that the string will continue.

Reminding students of their accumulated history prevents them from focusing on present behavior and directs their attention to the past. Since changing the past is impossible, you have locked students into a situation that has no escape. Release students from their past by eliminating mental scorekeeping from your language patterns. If you feel it is necessary to point out negative behaviors, confine your remarks to the present. Focus on what they are doing now.

"There you go again" works like a giant mirror. It is a style of speaking that reflects to students how we see them. It can be used to reflect negatively or positively.

"There you go again, another assignment in on time" is one example of using this phrase in a positive way. It helps the student create a picture in her head of herself as prompt with assignments. "There you go again, doing more than I required" encourages the child to picture herself as someone who goes beyond the minimum.

What you say following "There you go again" will give you data on how you are helping students see themselves. If leadership or honesty or lying or forgetfulness follows, be assured that you are inviting more of the same behavior into your classroom and into your students' lives.

Create a language assignment for yourself this week. Use "There you go again" in a positive way five times with students whose behaviors you want to reinforce. Celebrate as you notice how this phrase is enabling you to help your students see themselves in more positive ways. Congratulate yourself as you effectively use language to improve student self-esteem.

"You sure are persistent."

We used to believe that one's IQ was relatively fixed. From the time it could be measured, there was little we could do to raise it, no matter how much stimulation or education we provided. Now we know that one's IQ is variable and that through mental and emotional nourishment and education, there can be significant improvements. We also know that even with an increase in a student's IQ, there will be little change in his or her ability to succeed and be happy if the self-concept remains negative. Self-esteem, it seems, is as important to the educational process and quality of life as intelligence. In other words, a student's "I am's" are as important as their IQ's.

"I am's" are the beliefs that students hold about themselves. Many children have beliefs that are positive.

"I am capable."
"I am athletic."
"I am mathematical."
"I am worthwhile."
"I am a child of God."
"I am creative."
"I am responsible."

Likewise, many students hold negative beliefs about themselves.

"I am ugly."
"I am fat."
"I am uncoordinated."
"I am not wanted."
"I am stupid."
"I am not good enough."
"I am wrong."

"I am's" are formed early in life. Kindergarten teachers will tell you that their five-year-old students come to school with "I am's" already in place. These youngsters enter the formal educational process already holding firm beliefs about themselves. Some of these beliefs serve them well. *"I am attractive." "I can learn what I want to learn." "I am musical."* Others are erroneous or limiting. *"I* am dumb." "I am a troublemaker." "I am a klutz." Whether positive or negative, the self-beliefs that students hold at the beginning of kindergarten influence them throughout their entire lives. That is why we call them Life Sentences.

Life Sentences are critical because behavior flows from beliefs. If a student believes he is uncoordinated, he acts uncoordinated. Since that belief is firmly rooted in his consciousness, he is more likely to slip, trip or stumble than someone who believes he is athletic. The youngster who believes he is uncoordinated is also more likely to interpret events in ways that are consistent with that belief. The child's internal dialogue following a spilled glass of milk may be "There I go again, an uncoordinated klutz. That's the way I am." Over time he will prove to himself "I am uncoordinated."

Imagine two children approaching the task of riding a two-wheeled bike for the first time. One has the positive Life Sentence "I am athletic." The other has a negative Life Sentence "I am a klutz." The child with the negative Life Sentence approaches the bike tentatively. His eyes are cast downward. His step is slow and unsure. He touches the bike tentatively, suspiciously. His body language and behaviors all indicate "I can't." The child with the positive Life Sentence approaches the bike with confidence. There is power in his stride and strength in his grip of the handlebars. He is eager to begin. He acts as if he can.

Who do you believe will learn to ride the bike first? Which Life Sentence will be most helpful when learning this new skill?

Imagine the behaviors that will manifest themselves in your classroom when students believe "I am a slow learner," or when they believe "I catch on quickly." What kinds of behaviors do you think come from students who hold the Life Sentence "I am a leader," or "I am a troublemaker"? Who will learn math more quickly and easily, the child with an "I am capable" Life Sentence, or one believing "I am dumb"? You can see that Life Sentences are critical to students' success at creating their lives the way that they want them.

Life Sentences are formed early in life and may remain relatively fixed throughout. Still, teachers have great influence, because during childhood and adolescence Life Sentences are not yet firmly set in the consciousness. A skillful teacher can grant reprieves and commute Life Sentences by how he or she talks to students.

Teachers are like mirrors, constantly reflecting back to students what we think of them. Students sit in our classrooms, looking at those reflections and saying to themselves, "Oh, so that is what *I am*." We can strengthen or weaken a Life Sentence by the kinds of reflections that we send.

David Elkind tells a story about the day he accepted a negative Life Sentence during vocal music class. The teacher was preparing the children for a musical production. During practice she leveled a finger straight at young David Elkind and announced, "Elkind, you're a mouther." Since that time, David Elkind has held the belief that "I am not a singer." Our choice of language can positively or negatively affect the Life Sentences of our students. Thankfully, another one of young Elkind's teachers told him, "You have a flair for writing." That comment was one important contribution to what is certainly a Life Sentence of "I am a writer."

Recently, we overheard a fourth-grade teacher tell a student, "You sure are persistent."

"What is persistent?" asked the child.

"Persistent is what you were while you were learning your multiplication tables. You worked on your sixes over the weekend. You practiced them Monday night, Tuesday night, and Wednesday night. On Thursday you passed the skills test. You kept at it until you got it. That's persistent."

"Oh yea," said the ten year old as he walked away. "I sure am persistent."

As teachers we have minute-to-minute choices to make throughout every day about what behaviors to notice, what to mention, what to put under the magnifying glass. In every classroom there is evidence of cooperation and lack of cooperation. There are acts of responsibility and acts of irresponsibility. It is possible to see helpfulness or unhelpfulness, cooperation or a lack of cooperation. We decide what to see. We choose what we will mention and what we will reflect back to students.

These choices must be carefully made so that we have a positive influence on our students' Life Sentences.

"You always/never..."

Pay attention to the words *always* and *never*. Used indiscriminately, they can communicate negative expectations to your students.

"Why do you *always* interrupt me?"
"You *always* blame someone else."
"You *never* attempt to do anything extra."

When teachers use *always* and *never* to direct accusing statements at their students, they brand the students as being *that way*. Children who see themselves a certain way are more likely to act *that way*. The teacher talk that accompanies *always* and *never* actually reinforces the behavior that you want to eliminate.

Another problem for teachers who use *always* and *never* is that it diverts the student's attention away from the issue that needs to be dealt with and focuses it on the accusation. A typical internal response to "You always have to be first" is denial. The student remembers the one time, three years ago, when she chose to be last. She is now so busy thinking that she does not *always* have to be first, that she is unable to attend to the present problem.

When teachers remark, "You never give up" or "I can always count on you," students may be pleased with the praise, yet discredit the praiser. They may focus their attention on the validity of the statement rather than on the behavior which was endorsed. Students know that *always/never* statements are not true. Sometimes they do give up. Sometimes they are not dependable. If they determine that the statement is a fallacy, they may discredit the speaker as well as the statement. Their self-talk might be:

"She's pretty dumb."
"Don't believe anything he says."
"She doesn't know me very well."
"Somehow I fooled him into thinking that I'm something I'm not."

When you wish to communicate positive expectancy by praising in this manner, we suggest that you use the

58

words *usually* and *most of the time.* "I can usually depend on this class for tons of creative ideas." "Most of the time I get so many different ideas from this group, that I have trouble choosing one." Now your teacher talk is consistent with reality and helps students focus on the positive message you want to send.

Sometimes students often imitate our use of *always* and *never.*

"She always strikes out."
"He never passes the ball to me."
"He never stops talking about himself."
"He always gives homework."

Students use these words when they are complaining or disowning.

"You never give me a chance, Mr. White."
"You always let that row go first."

You can help students hear that their statements are all-inclusive generalizations by asking, "What do you mean, 'always'?" "What do you mean, 'never'?" These gentle questions will help students to refocus on what they really mean.

"I want a turn, Mr. White."
"Can our row go first this time?"

Free your teacher talk from sweeping generalizations like *always* and *never* when giving students feedback. Save *always* and *never* for the few instances when they are accurate descriptors.

"You sure are lucky."

There are many words and phrases in our language that refer to the concept of luck. Some of the more common terms are *good fortune, chance,* and *coincidence.* Phrases include: *"You're jinxed; What an unfortunate string of events; I guess it wasn't in the cards; That's fate."*

When you use the language of luck with students, you embellish the myth that luck is at work in their lives. This style of language diminishes their sense of personal power. It gives some outside force (luck) credit for success and failure. It dilutes their understanding of cause and effect, and encourages them to disown the role they play in their own success.

Rachael, age six, worked for twenty minutes building a tower of blocks. After several trials and errors, she created a structure that surpassed her own expectation. Excited about the accomplishment, Rachael showed it to her teacher. The teacher missed an opportunity to mention Rachael's perseverance, sense of balance and effort. He nodded admiringly and said, "You're lucky it's still standing."

Charles spent three nights at the city library. He logged ten hours of pouring through the periodical files, looking for references for his term paper. When he told his senior English teacher about the five new sources he found, the teacher remarked, "You really lucked out at the library."

"You sure were in the right place at the right time; You're leading a charmed life; What a coincidence; You stumbled onto a good one there" are more examples of the language of luck. This language encourages students to discount the importance of preparation, skill, effort and persistence. They disown the power that they do have and give it away to fate, fortune, or coincidence.

Life appears, in one sense, to be an ongoing mixture of good and bad breaks. Yet, perhaps it is really adequate or inadequate preparation, abundance or lack of skills, recognizing many or few alternatives, responding to or disregarding opportunities. How a student chooses to see opportunities, which opportunities he chooses to take advantage of, and the skills and preparation that student brings with him are responsible for success. Drop the language of luck from your vocabulary and help your students feel the power, self-reliance and control they have in their own lives.

"Okay, who did it?"

Teachers ask "Who did it?" in order to gain information, but this question gives more information than it gets. If answered accurately it gets the name of an offender. At the same time it tells students that the teacher cares about finding fault and fixing blame. It identifies that teacher as someone who cares more about punishment than the search for solutions.

"Who did it?" is beside the point. It draws attention to *who* is the problem rather than *what* is the problem. It creates a loser and brands someone as wrong. It serves to keep the teacher focused on blame instead of seeking solutions.

"Who left the paint brushes in the sink?" does not give students information about the teacher's feelings. It does not focus on what needs to be done *now*. It gives them no clues as to what behaviors the teacher expects in the future. It is not a teaching tool, but a prelude to punishment. One variation, "Okay, who's fault was it?" is especially unhelpful. Two second-grade girls recently answered this question by pointing to each other. This style of teacher language encourages students to live out a "me vs. them" attitude. It invites them to do self-preservation at the expense of others.

As an alternative, we suggest teachers describe the situation and state their feelings. "I see paint brushes in the sink and I'm angry." "I notice paint on the carpet and I'm irritated." It is also useful in these situations to give students information. "The paint just spilled. We can use a sponge." "When paint gets spilled, it stains."

When teachers share their feelings, describe the situation and provide information, they send a different message. The message is that they believe students are intelligent enough to choose an appropriate action once they have the necessary information.

Next time you hear yourself say, "Who did it?" – stop. Question your own motives. What is more important, identifying the culprit or focusing on what needs to be done? Let your words reflect your answer.

"Tell me your side of it."

Sides exist in competitive games, courtrooms and war. They have no place in collaborative classrooms where connectedness, belonging, and oneness are encouraged. *Side* is the key word here. If there is one side, there must be another. This hints that someone is right and someone is wrong, and serves to strengthen adversarial relationships. "Tell me your side of it" pits one child against another. It promotes a "me vs. you" mind-set that encourages people to put distance between each other and their positions. It communicates separateness and invites polarization.

An alternative to "Tell me your side of it" is to ask students to share their perception, or help you appreciate their thinking. "How did you see that?" "How does it seem to you?" or "What was your thinking?" are examples of this type of teacher language.

When we ask students to communicate their thinking, they will describe many thought processes, rationales, and conclusions. When those differences are listened to and acknowledged, students learn that different ideas can stand side by side. The existence of one does not have to eliminate the other.

When two or more students are asked, "How did you see that?" there will be a variety of responses. None are wrong. Each child is an expert on how he or she viewed a situation. Even though their perceptions, thoughts, and beliefs conflict, all views need to be respected and treated as part of the whole.

Cooperation, feelings of connectedness, and mutual respect are necessary ingredients for building effective classrooms. These concepts can be promoted in your classroom by choosing language that helps students see that, in reality, we are all on the same side *together*.

"Did you win?"

After Kathryn's track meet, Amy's debate, Elizabeth's softball game, and Dorothy's defense of first-chair trumpet, each girl's teacher asked, "Did you win?"

Kathryn came in last in the hundred-yard dash.
Elizabeth's team lost the game by one run.
Amy's team took second place at the debate.
Dorothy successfully defended her band position.

Because each teacher directed his interest toward winning, he missed an opportunity to help his student focus on the many joys and satisfactions of competition. According to traditional thought, only one of these girls won; Dorothy. In our society, there is a pervasive belief that each event, competition, or category can applaud only one winner. In fact, there is a world-wide obsession with being first, so it is crucial for teachers to seize opportunities to help students focus on events instead of outcomes, and move attention to the pleasures of participating.

The obsession to be first separates, and creates unrealistic expectations and demands on competitors. During the Winter Olympics we watched a young man agonize because he had lost the downhill ski competition. The announcer referred to him as a loser. In fact, he had missed skiing the fastest downhill run *ever*, by two hundredths of a second. *Hundredths* of a second! A loser?

We know an eighth grader who refused to go out for track, because people might ridicule him for running too slowly. "But *you* are out there running," we argued. "*They* are just sitting there! You deserve admiration no matter what your time or place." He shook his head. "But I won't win." He chose to give up an opportunity to be with his friends, have fun, and gain attention from his peers because he was afraid to lose.

Chick runs ten-kilometer road races. Our five-year-old does not understand that Chick "wins" whether he finishes first or four hundredth. We know Chick wins if he has fun, meets new friends, enjoys a sunny day or a warm rain. He wins when he finishes the race and feels the support of cheering spectators. He wins when he achieves his timing goal, or sets a new record for himself. He wins with improved health, and self-esteem that flows from the self-discipline and commitment of daily runs. No matter how we explain, Geoffrey does not understand. Already, he has caught "must win fever." We tell him, "Yes, Chick won. And he wasn't first."

In order to be happy and successful, children must learn to deal effectively with competition. They must learn to accept "wins" *and* "losses" with the grace that comes from understanding that wins are only part of the pleasure of competition. Camaraderie, testing oneself, belonging, effort, and learning are all important parts of the competitive process. Winning does not necessarily mean being "first." We can begin to communicate this to students by asking, "What did you like about it?"

"What did you like about it?" is a processing question. It asks students to consider various aspects of the competition. It asks that they focus on the pleasurable ones. People tend to notice what they do not like about any activity, and it is important that they notice what they *do* like. Students develop thinking skills as they reconstruct the competition in their minds, analyzing and evaluating.

Relationships develop and expand, because "What did you like about it?" requires more than a one-word response. Dialogue is encouraged as students elaborate on activities and converse with the teacher about interests.

We believe that many students miss countless opportunities to develop talents, learn, and have fun because they are afraid they will not win. Kathryn was a winner because she *ran* the hundred-yard dash. Elizabeth won because she has developed her skills to a level where she has been asked to join a traditionally all-male baseball team. Amy is a winner because she used to be afraid to speak in class, and now does so effortlessly and skillfully. Dorothy is a winner too, not because she beat the opposition, but because she had never played as well as she did while defending her first chair, and she knows it. All students are capable of winning and feeling like winners, if society's obsession with being first does not rob them of experiencing themselves that way.

Teachers can help students move beyond this limited and limiting view of competition by changing "Did you win?" to "What did you like about it?"

"How can you both get what you want?"

Jesse and Jamie were partners for a seventh-grade social studies report. They were expected to work together. During the time their teacher gave for partners to collaborate, a heated discussion erupted. It threatened to turn into a full-blown argument.

"Why won't you ever cooperate?" Jamie accused.

"Everything always has to be your way!" Jesse slung back. A classroom crisis was in the making.

The teacher approached the boys calmly and commented, "Looks as if you have a problem."

"We have to go to the library to work!"

"I want to work in the room!"

The teacher put a calming hand on both students' shoulders. "What is it that you want, Jamie?"

"I want to go to the library!"

"Say some more."

"We only have three sources and we are supposed to have six."

"What is it that *you* want, Jesse?" the teacher asked the other student without commenting on the first explanation.

"I don't want to go to the library. I have band next hour and if I have to go to band all the way from the library, I'll be late."

"What *do* you want?" the teacher persisted.

"I want to be on time for band."

"So *you* want to be on time for band and *Jamie* wants more sources for the report," the teacher summarized. "The question is, how can you both get what you want? Please talk about that and see if you can find an answer that is acceptable to both of you," she told them. "I'll check with you later." Then she turned and walked away.

A short time later, the students approached their teacher. Both looked satisfied and appeared to be friendly. Jesse spoke. "We're going to the library for half an hour and then we're coming back so Jamie won't be late for band."

The teacher smiled affirmation. "Glad you worked it out." Later she would process with the students how they were able to solve the problem together once they had redefined it. Jesse really did not mind going to the library.

That was not his real problem. His real concern was being late for band. Jamie did not really care whether they worked in the library or in the classroom. He simply wanted to have more sources for the report. This solution worked for both. Neither student had to give up anything; both got what they wanted.

"How can you both get what you want?" is a strategy that builds interdependence and encourages cooperation. It helps children work together to redefine problems and search for acceptable solutions.

The dictionary defines cooperation as "working together toward a common end." The important words here are "together" and "common." "How can you both get what you want?" helps children work on a problem together to find a common solution.

Children in conflict usually focus on "winning" an encounter because experience has taught them that compromise means giving up what they want. Compromise means that everybody loses something. Even the most altruistic child is unwilling to compromise if it means always losing part of what she wants.

"How can you both get what you want?" helps children redefine problems in terms of wants and needs instead of winners and losers. It opens up options where previously there seemed to be none. It encourages cooperation, so *everyone* wins. You can help your students see that they can work together to solve problems and together they can win. The next time students seem deadlocked on an issue, show your confidence and support by asking, "How can you both get what you want?"

"What *will* you do?"

Each of the following statements represents a student's honest desire to change an undesirable behavior.

"I won't hit him anymore."
"I won't be late again."
"I won't pass notes third hour."

Teachers can help turn these positive *intentions* into positive *actions* by inviting students to think about and articulate alternative behaviors. Ask them, "What *will* you do?" This question moves students' thinking from what they will *not* do (hitting, coming to class late, or passing notes) to what they *will* do instead.

"I won't hit him anymore" or "I won't be late again" are easy answers that students feed us to get themselves off the hook. Our suggested phrase "What will you do?" forces them to pause and think about positive behaviors. It shifts their attention from the easy "won't do" statements to more serious thought about helpful alternatives.

"What will you do?" is an invitation to students to articulate a plan of action that focuses on the positive. By stating that plan aloud, commitment is strengthened and the student is more likely to put his plan into action.

"What will you do?" is a helpful question to ask *yourself* as you implement the ideas in this book. When you seem to be stuck in old language patterns that no longer feel comfortable, use the question to clarify your thoughts and intentions. Your language will change as you focus on defining what you will do.

"Act as if."

All teachers work with students who take an "I can't" stance towards learning for some portion of the day. These students think they can't, believe they can't, and act as if they can't. They even talk as if they can't. Teachers hear "I can't" talk all the time:

> "I can't do it!"
> "I don't get it!"
> "I can't."

How do you respond when one of your students looks up and says, "I can't do it"? Many teachers reply, "Sure, you can, come on, *try*." Teachers believe that if students try, they will prove to themselves that they can. It sounds logical but it does not work. Typically, students respond with "I'm trying." Neither the teacher nor the student realizes that trying does not work. *Doing* works. "Try" is too often used as an excuse for giving up. Anybody busy *trying* is not busy *doing*.

We recommend "Act as if" as a strategy to get your students doing rather than trying. The next time one of your students looks up to you and whines, "I can't do it," resist telling them to try. Say instead, "I want you to 'act as if' you already know how to do this." Then step back and watch what happens. We predict that you will be delighted as most students move away from the "I can't" stance and begin doing.

In the early grades, "pretend" or "Play like you can" works as well as "Act as if." A kindergarten teacher recently told us that she uses these terms interchangeably. When her students are stuck, she tells them, "Play like you can" and "Pretend you know how." Soon they are busy doing.

A middle school science teacher reported this incident. "I approached two students who appeared to be stuck on a lab exercise. They complained that they didn't know what to do next. I asked, 'What would you do if you did know?' When they answered, I replied, 'Why not do that, then?' They did, got unstuck and moved ahead. It's amazing how well the "act as if" philosophy works."

A high school foreign language teacher reported that one of her students panicked right before the semester final. He froze and could not remember the steps to the folk dance he was about to perform. "Fake it" was her reply. To her delight, the student began to "act as if" and soon remembered the dance routine.

Whether you say "pretend," "fake it," or any other variation of "act as if," the results are the same. Students start doing and it is only then that correction, guidance, and constructive feedback are possible.

Although encouraging students to "try" sometimes gets results, you will be more successful with "act as if" and "pretend." One reason is that "acting as if" is more playful, less serious and stressful. Trying implies struggle, while pretending is fun. Some students will not even try because if they do not succeed they consider it failure. If they *pretend* and do not make it, there is no stigma or failure attached.

"Act as if" can change your life. Do you want more energy in the classroom? Act as if you have energy. Do you want to be more positive about your professional practice? Act as if you are positive. Do you want to use "Teacher Talk" effectively? *Act as if you can.*

"It's easy."

Barbara sat hunched over, gripping her pencil tightly. Sighs of exasperation revealed her frustration with long division. Barbara's teacher observed her efforts closely, then decided to intervene. Desiring to encourage the student and communicate his faith in her abilities and intelligence, Barbara's teacher explained the process of long division. Then he whispered, "Come on, Barbara, you can do it. *It's easy*." He did not know that these simple words of encouragement had trapped Barbara in a no-win situation.

The teacher who encourages with "It's easy" may initiate feelings of fear in the student. Barbara is afraid of appearing incompetent. "He says it's easy," she says to herself. "What if I can't do it? Everyone will think I'm stupid."

By putting her faith in her teacher's words, "It's easy," Barbara may lose faith in herself. If she attempts the task because she trusts her teacher and wants to please him, she risks failure. Failing at something "easy," she may feel discouraged and hopeless. She is liable to tell herself, "What's the use of doing anything in school? I can't even do something easy. I must be stupid."

On the other hand, Barbara may utilize the teacher's words to get herself started. She may breeze through the long division and discover that it *was* easy for her. What amount of satisfaction can she feel for completing a task that was already pronounced *easy*? She will probably feel only relief that she was able to do it, and did not appear foolish. "Of course I did it" goes her internal dialogue. "Anybody can do it. After all, it's easy."

A different possibility is that Barbara may complete the task successfully, but with great difficulty. Instead of feeling proud, she may believe that a difficult task would be beyond her ability, because she had to struggle to complete something *easy*. Since "easy" tasks are hard for her, she may question her own intelligence. Her self-talk may be "Even if I work my hardest, I can only do something easy. I must be stupid."

In each of these situations, Barbara can only lose by attempting a task that the teacher has pronounced "easy."

When you want students to *win*, and you wish to communicate your faith in them, we suggest that you change "It's easy" to "I think you're ready for this."

"I think you're ready for this" does not address the difficulty of the task. That interpretation is left to the student. The phrase communicates the teacher's opinion of the child's skill level *at that time*, regardless of the degree of difficulty the child attaches to the task. If the child succeeds, she can say to herself, "I was ready for this. I did it!" She can enjoy the accomplishment and experience satisfaction according to her own assessment of how hard she worked. If she does not succeed, she can say, "I guess I'm not ready for this, *yet*," comforted by the teacher's confidence and her own assurance that she will be successful in the future when she *is* ready.

Your choice of language helps students create self-talk that affirms their capabilities and strengthens their self-esteem. You can communicate faith in their competence and encourage their efforts. Eliminate "It's easy" from your teacher talk. We think you are ready for this.

"I'm proud of you."

Participants who attend our "Teacher Talk" seminars are often surprised to hear some of our recommendations regarding phrases detailed in this book. At no time, however, do their faces reveal greater surprise than when we suggest they drop "I'm proud of you" from their verbal repertoire. "What can be wrong with this one?" they wonder.

We believe that "I'm proud of you" is somewhat condescending. The speaker takes the role of evaluator and assumes the right to judge the accomplishment or the person who achieved it. The judge looks down and pronounces, "I'm proud of you." This language gives us the flavor of the master patting the well-behaved puppy on the head.

We believe you can strengthen the phrase "I'm proud of you," and create the positive effects you intend by changing one word. Replace *of* with *for*. Instead of "I'm proud *of* you," the statement becomes "I'm proud *for* you."

Say this revised phrase out loud. "I'm proud for you." Hear the subtle difference. You may want to say this one several times while alternating *of* and *for*. Tune into your feelings as you speak.

"I'm proud *for* you" keeps the focus on the doer. The speaker appreciates and communicates pleasure in the other person's accomplishment. Attention and credit go to the doer.

Imagine that you wrote us a letter detailing your reaction to this book. Think about how you would choose to feel as you read our letter of response informing you that we are very proud of your ability to articulate your thoughts. "Who are *they* to judge *me*?" might be your reaction. Indeed, who are *we* to be proud of *you*? It is up to you to be proud of you if you choose, for reasons you alone determine.

"I'm tired of seeing you behave this way."

This phrase is intended to send the message "I don't like that behavior." It signals students that the teacher is unhappy with their behavior and wants them to change it. We suggest that teachers use this phrase instead, as a signal to do a bit of inner exploration. Perhaps they can begin to see things differently.

You see, each of us has a different way of seeing.

Recently we arranged for several teachers to observe in classrooms where the cooperative learning model was being implemented. All of the teachers watched the same lesson, the same student reaction, and the same outcome. Each *reported* seeing something different. Some teachers saw noisy groups. Others perceived a productive hum. Some saw disorganization and chaos. Others described freedom within structure.

These teachers saw things differently because people do not see through their eyes only. We see through the filters of our beliefs, values, ideas, attitudes, and total life experiences. We all see through the filters of our past experiences and interpret what we see in our own unique way.

This phenomenon occurs in whatever we see. We look at an event and project onto it whatever it is we have within us. Some people see a good day, while others see a bad day. However, it is the same day. Some see student X as a troublemaker, others as a potential leader. It is the same student. How we see something or someone tells more about *us* than it does about who or what we saw. It tells about our beliefs, attitudes, and values. It tells what we have been projecting outward.

Perception is a choice. How we see students is not fixed. Our perceptions are flexible and under our control. It is possible to see students as troublemakers or as crying out for help. We can perceive cheaters or see students who do not yet know that learning has more value than getting right answers. We can see students as mouthy or as young people struggling to get their social needs met.

Perception is critical, because how you see what goes on in your classroom affects how you react to it. If you choose to see kids cheating on a test as awful, you are more likely to blame and punish. If you see cheating as an opportunity to help students learn that mastering concepts is more important than accumulating right answers, you are more likely to use problem-solving techniques. If you notice students struggling with group work and perceive them as incompetent, you are likely to behave as an interventionist, either solving the problem or stopping the group work. If you perceive the struggle as an opportunity for groups to learn about working together, you are likely to behave as an interactionist, pointing out situations and turning problems back to the group for solutions.

"I don't like what I'm seeing" or "I'm tired of seeing you behave this way" can serve as a caution to you. It is one indication that you are choosing to see students in a negative light.

Often, we define students by their actions. We label them as troublemakers, liars, procrastinators, complainers, or reluctant learners. In order to be of help to them, we need to learn to see beyond their act to their essence.

Troublemakers are just doing their troublemaker act. Reluctant students are doing their reluctant act. Bullies are doing their bully act. But that is not the essence of their real selves. It is not the truth about them. It is just an act. We are all much more than our act. All of us are valuable in our own right, regardless of our act. No matter how unskilled our behavior, our intent is to solicit love and acceptance.

If *we* do not see beyond students' acts, who will? If *we* do not communicate to them that in spite of their acts, we see their worth shining through, who will?

"I don't like what I'm seeing here" can be a signal to you that you have lost sight of the student's real worth. Whether you say it aloud or silently, hear it as a sign that it is time to question how you are perceiving your students. Ask yourself, "How am I seeing this?" or "How am I seeing these students?" If you do not like the answers you find and are dissatisfied with your perceptions, ask for help. Go to the quiet place within yourself. Center yourself. Touch that place where you tap your inner knowing, and ask, "How else can I see this? What else can I be seeing here? How can I see this differently?"

Find a way of seeing what you do like; one that leaves you feeling peaceful, secure, and full of renewed respect and acceptance for all your students.

Whenever you hear yourself announcing, "I don't like what I'm seeing," take yourself seriously. While you may or may not insist on changes in the students, insist on change within yourself. If you do not like what you are seeing, then choose to see it another way.

"How can we see this differently?"

When a student is agonizing over some perceived injustice, encourage him to consider another point of view by asking, "How can we see this differently?"

When a difficult situation must be endured, help students to experience peace of mind through acceptance of the inevitable by asking, "How can we see this differently?"

When the class is indignant about a situation, encourage tolerance and defenselessness by asking, "How can we see this differently?"

Students in conflict tend to get caught up in their own point of view. They develop tunnel vision and can see things only one way. Their beliefs become truths to them, and their perceptions become facts.

One seventh-grade homeroom teacher was confronted by several students who were upset with their second semester schedules. A self-awareness, self-exploration program for junior high students had replaced gym on their schedules for the first eight weeks of the second semester. "It's unfair," the seventh graders complained. "We hate this junk. We want gym." This teacher began the process of moving these students towards developing more open-mindedness by asking, "How can we see this differently?"

In the class discussion which followed, students brainstormed possible ways to perceive the situation in which they found themselves; how to "change their minds" even if they couldn't change the situation. Some of their ideas follow:

"Well, we sure will appreciate gym more when we get it."
"At least this new class is something different."
"It's probably better than math."
"We could view it as a challenge."

Students learned through this exercise in perception that it is possible to see the same thing from different angles. When students learn that opposing ideas can stand together, they have taken an important step towards effective problem solving and conflict resolution.

The phrase "How can we see this differently?" can remind you, the teacher, of the importance of shifting perspective. One teacher we know used this phrase to reduce stress during her thirty-minute lunch period. She had just begun her one duty-free period of the day when she heard a knock on the lunchroom door.

As she opened the door, she immediately recognized two of her fourth graders held firmly by the playground supervisor. "This one hit this one," began the lunch hour aide, "and then this one kicked him back." With that he deposited the two students at the door, turned, and left.

"This is miserable!" muttered the teacher to herself. "Now, I won't even get a chance to relax during lunch." She felt disgruntled and helpless; totally victimized. Then she recognized that this was an opportunity to change her own mind *even if she could not change the situation.* She employed this suggested piece of teacher talk by taking a deep breath and asking herself, "How can I see this differently?" Within seconds she answered herself. "This is an opportunity to help these students learn problem-solving skills. I'd rather do it later, and it's happening now. I can handle it."

Seeing this situation as an opportunity instead of as a disaster, this teacher was able to respond effectively. She put down her lunch, went to the two boys and helped them define their problem. Once the problem was defined, she asked them to generate a list of solutions and pick one on which they could both agree. She told them to let her know when they had finished, and she returned to her lunch. She was able to relax and enjoy her duty-free lunch period, as well as her lunch, knowing that she had chosen to view the situation in a way that was helpful to everyone concerned.

Whenever you feel exasperated, frustrated, or without hope, ask yourself, "How can I see this differently?" Take a moment to relax and take a deep breath. Trust that an answer, *your* answer, will come. It will enable you to shift your perception to a less stressful, more constructive view.

"How can we see this differently?" will help both teachers and students remember that even when circumstances must be endured, we *can* change our perception. We can experience these inevitable situations without stress and distress by learning to see them differently.

"Some of us..."

Some of us are in the band.
Some of us play sports.
Some of us do our assignments.
Some of us like cafeteria food.
Some of us are on the honor roll.

When we see students running through the halls, copying from other students' papers, or calling each other names, we may be tempted to criticize or categorize in ways which separate us from students and elevate us to a superior position.

"Some of us..." reminds teachers of our connectedness to our students and of our common humanity. It is inclusive language which prevents us from creating a *me vs. them* atmosphere in our classrooms. It communicates to students that we are each an important individual part of a greater whole. It moves students away from I/Me/My thinking towards the holistic view of Us/We/Our.

When we say "some of us," our language helps us connect with students by focusing attention on our commonalities. We help our students and ourselves create attitudes of unity in which we sense the whole or see our part in it. We are able to learn together harmoniously as we leave behind a *"me vs. them"* consciousness and expand our vision to a *"we together"* view of the world.

"You did a good job."

Praise is the number one behavior modification tool employed by educators. Teachers tell us that praise motivates students, builds self-confidence, and improves their self-esteem. The assumption is that praise is helpful. Yet, what if it is a false assumption? Perhaps praise is not the esteem builder that we have always believed.

"You did a *good* job" is one example of *evaluative* praise. Others include:

"You're a *terrific* speller."
"That's a *beautiful* picture."
"I think it's *wonderful.*"
"Fantastic!"

Evaluative praise evaluates. When you praise someone in this way you rate them with words like good, excellent, super, tremendous, fantastic, and superb. In each case your words represent a judgment of what you think about the other person. Your praise is a judgmental interpretation of their behavior, accomplishments, ideas, appearance, or character.

Some teachers protest. "Yes, but evaluative praise helps students feel *good!* What's wrong with that?"

Evaluative praise helps the person being praised to feel good *temporarily.* In that sense, it works very much like a drug. It helps people feel good for the moment and leaves them longing for more. Children are especially susceptible to the dependency induced by heavy doses of evaluative praise.

A frustrated art teacher once explained how she tried to wean praise-dependent children off evaluative praise by describing and appreciating their work. A child would finish a project, bring it to her, and initiate the following discussion:

Student: How do you like my picture? Is it good?
Teacher: I appreciate the diversity of your design.
Student: But is it good?
Teacher: Tell me what *you* think about it.
Student: I like it, but I want to know if it's good.

The above conversation is not atypical. It happens continually in classrooms, initiated by students hooked on evaluative praise and looking for a quick fix. Students have learned to depend on others for their measures of success. They see others as the major source of approval in their lives, and they have come to "need" a regular shot of evaluative praise to maintain their sense of worth. These students want others to tell them they are *good, excellent, beautiful,* or *wonderful.* Without the constant reminders, evaluative praise-dependent children are uncomfortable and insecure. They do not know how to praise themselves. Excessive use of evaluative praise has reinforced a tendency to look away from themselves for evidence of their competence. They cannot enjoy an accomplishment unless somebody is around to approve of it. They rely on others for proof of their importance and ability, and do not develop an adequate internal standard of self-worth. Evaluative praise encourages students to take their self-image from others' perceptions and to become dependent on someone else's opinion or approval.

The art teacher in the previous anecdote *can* succeed in weaning her students from evaluative praise, and it will take time and perseverance. Teachers looking for ways to help their students develop self-confidence, self-esteem and self-motivation will not find evaluative praise helpful. The alternatives we suggest are *descriptive* and *appreciative* praise, detailed on the following pages.

"All your letters are right between the lines."

This phrase is an example of descriptive praise. Descriptive praise describes accomplishments or situations and affirms rather than evaluates what has been done. Examples follow:

> "The floor is clear of litter. I am pleased that we will be ready to go today when the bell rings."
> "Your report listed at least three rationales for each point you made. You followed the directions exactly."
> "Your beginning sentence caught my interest and I wanted to read on."

Notice the absence of evaluation in descriptive praise. You will not find words like good, excellent, or great. Instead, we chose words that describe the situation and allow the students to draw their own conclusions. In this way, students evaluate themselves.

There are two parts of praise. The first part is the phrase that is actually spoken. The second part is the self-talk of the person to whom the praise is directed. It is the second part, i.e. what the person says to herself about the praise, that has the most beneficial effect on self-esteem, self-responsibility, and internal motivation.

When teachers praise descriptively, "You have seventeen out of eighteen correct and showed all of your work," they leave room for the student to draw his own conclusion. He says to himself, "I did a good job," or "This is an excellent paper." The evaluation is internal and is given by a person the child believes: himself. When the praise is believed, self-esteem goes up.

When students develop an internal standard of excellence, they produce excellence more often. When they can judge their efforts against their own personal standards, their ability to improve school work increases. This is because they have clear ideas of academic goals and a personal commitment to achieving those goals. How do students develop internal standards and become self-directed? They do it by breaking their dependence on evaluation from adults and by learning to rely on themselves for evaluation of their accomplishments. They learn, through many experiences of teacher-provided *descriptive* praise, to evaluate themselves.

If you want to help your students develop an internal standard of excellence, as well as improved self-esteem, motivation and self-responsibility, begin to change your praise from evaluation to description. When you hear yourself saying (or see yourself writing) "good job," ask yourself, "Just what is good about it? Is the spelling accurate? Is the handwriting between the lines? Is each paragraph indented? What is it, specifically, about this paper, report, project, or effort that I think is good?" Then relate it descriptively.

Resist writing "excellent" on the top of a report. Write instead "The order of events you listed were accurate. Each point supported your major thesis."

Erase "very good" from the mechanical drawing. Replace it with "Your attention to detail on figure B was precise and went beyond the minimum criteria."

Catch yourself saying "good job" to students following reading groups. Rephrase your teacher talk to describe the situation. "You stayed on task today and most of you finished your boardwork. Not one person interrupted me and we finished ahead of schedule."

Monitor your students' reaction to your new style of praising. Watch their expressions as they tell *themselves* "I did a good job," "My report was good," and "My drawing was superb." Realize that your skillful way of speaking with students has an important positive impact of their lives.

"I appreciate your efforts. Thanks."

Appreciative praise is another helpful alternative to evaluation. This style of praise tells the student what behavior is helpful, explains any positive effects, and shares appreciation.

"Thank you for offering to help check papers.
That takes a load off my back."

"I was happy to see the sink cleaned out.
Now I don't have to do it before I go home. Thanks."

With appreciative praise, the teacher makes a statement and the student is able to draw her own conclusion. For example, the teacher says, "Thank you for collecting the books. That saved me ten minutes." The student concludes "I really helped out." The teacher's words are "Your help with the movie projector enabled me to get the class started on time today. Thanks!" The student's self-talk is "I can make a difference. I'm worthwhile." In each case the teacher's words leave room for the child to make the evaluation.

When using appreciative praise it is important to comment on specific acts. If you tell students that you appreciate their honesty, dependability, or promptness, go on to describe specifically the ways in which they acted dependable, honest or prompt. A comment like "I appreciate you being here exactly when you said you would" allows the student to say to herself, "I am dependable."

Begin to strengthen your praise by paying attention to it. Examine the comments you write on students' papers. Monitor what you say. When you feel tempted to evaluate, ask yourself, "How can I arrange my words so they can draw their own conclusions? What can I say so students can evaluate themselves?" The act of praising is a skill. It can be developed *and* improved.

"That's terrible."

Criticism and praise are closely related. They are flip sides of the same coin. Criticism, like praise, can be delivered in evaluative, descriptive or appreciative terms. Terrible, ugly, sloppy, poor, disgusting, and awful are examples of criticism that evaluates. Evaluative criticism ("The report was terrible" or "That's a poor effort"), like evaluative praise, gives the student little useful information. It is not helpful for the student to know that the report was terrible unless he knows specifically why you think so. It is of little benefit for the child to know her effort was poor, unless she knows exactly what was poor. Without specific knowledge she cannot correct mistakes or learn from them.

If you tell a student that his information was inaccurate in three places, you give him information he can use to improve the report. When you show him the four misspelled words and the two run-on sentences, he will know *why* you thought it was poor. When you are *descriptive* with your feedback, giving specific information about what you dislike and why, the student has valuable information from which to learn. However, if our comments are evaluative, the child is left wondering what it was that was not good enough.

Sharing displeasure or giving information about what you would appreciate in the future is another way to give students specific feedback. Examples include:

> "I don't like cleaning up the sink before I go home. I would appreciate it if the brushes are cleaned out and put away next time."
> "I'd appreciate a name in the upper left-hand corner next time."
> "I like it best when you leave the reading corner the way you found it before you used it. Books belong on the shelf."

Students generally respond better when you share what you would appreciate or describe what you do not like, than they do if you criticize with evaluation. You will get a more positive response by stating, "Milk cartons belong in the waste basket. I don't enjoy seeing them left on the lunchroom table" than you will by saying, "This lunchroom is awful." You will encourage greater cooperation when your remarks are "I don't enjoy being interrupted" than when you say, "You're rude and inconsiderate."

Students often hear feedback that evaluates as an attack. They believe it is aimed directly at them and they take it personally. Resentment, resistance and defensiveness follow. If you learn to speak to the situation instead of the person, *what* was done rather than *who* did it, there is less chance that students will take offense. Choose words that focus on what was or was not accomplished, what is included or is missing in the assignment, what you *specifically* like or dislike.

"The report was incomplete. There is no summary of the points" focuses on the report and specifically describes the problem. "You did a lousy job" draws attention to the person and does not offer instruction.

"It's 10:15 and the meeting has started" speaks to the situation. "You're late" points to the person.

"You didn't make it long enough" puts the spotlight on the person. "The paper falls short of the two-hundred word requirement" points to the product.

Listen to your criticism in the weeks ahead. Become increasingly aware of how you communicate negative feedback to students. When you hear yourself evaluating, stop. Recall the rules of criticism: *Speak to the situation and describe it specifically.* Rephrase your negative feedback. Choose words that will educate rather than evaluate.

"That's not a good excuse."

Teachers often inform students, "That's not a good excuse." By giving them feedback on what we think of their excuses, we believe that we are teaching them to behave more responsibly. Actually, our words have the opposite effect.

When we determine the acceptability of a student's excuse, we set ourselves up as judge. We communicate to the students that our role is one of excuse-examiner. Therefore, it is our job to pass judgment on their excuses. That leaves them the role of excuse-givers and encourages them to generate excuses for us to rate.

When we say, "That's not a good excuse," we communicate "If you had a good excuse, I might accept it. If I accept your excuse, then you will be *excused* from responsibility or consequences." Every time this happens we undermine student responsibility and actually invite excuses. Students are thus encouraged to spend their time and energy creating excuses for the teacher instead of taking action to rectify the situation.

When we use language that accepts or rejects excuses, students see *us* as responsible for their actions. If we listen to an excuse for unfinished homework and reject it as not good enough, they believe *we* are the cause of their lowered grade. If we consider and then deny their excuse for turning in their term paper late, *we* are seen as responsible. If we judge their excuse for not returning the field trip permission slip, students see *us* as determining whether or not they go on the trip. They see *us* as having the power to determine whether or not they experience the field trip, get an acceptable score, or pass the test. They come to believe that *we* are responsible for whether or not each situation turns out the way they want.

We suggest that you use teacher talk that keeps you from passing judgment on the excuse. Help students own their behavior and assume more responsibility for it by using language that focuses on consequences and on the role students play in creating them. When a student offers the excuse "I know I'm late, but my locker wouldn't open," reply, "I'm glad you're here and this is your third tardy. When you come late three times, you choose to stay an extra hour after school." When a child wants to be excused from returning the field trip permission slip on time because father was out of town, direct your remarks to the consequence. "When you fail to return the permission slip, you choose to miss the field trip." When a student begins excuses for not turning in homework, refuse to get caught up in evaluating the reasons *even when they seem reasonable.* Reply matter-of-factly with "Missing homework assignments require make-up work. You've chosen to participate in study hall on Thursday after school."

Students will usually not back off after the first excuse. They will persist in an effort to make you responsible for the outcome. "I couldn't help it," they will argue. "I just couldn't get my lock to work!" "It's not my fault that my dad went on a business trip and couldn't sign my permission slip!" Resist the temptation to acknowledge the excuse. Continue with your lesson.

Language that refuses to acknowledge excuses sends students helpful messages. They learn that your role is not that of judging excuses and that their behavior is more important to you than excuses. You teach them through experience that even when life seems unfair or seems to deal them a bad hand, *they can handle it.*

It is very important to us, as teachers, to feel that we are fair with students, so we often enter into the excuse game with the positive intention that students feel heard and understood. Paradoxically, it is the teachers who "bend over backwards" to be fair by hearing excuses and ruling on them, who are perceived by students as showing favoritism. Because these teachers acknowledge excuses by listening and ruling on them, the students who are ruled against are likely to believe the teacher is unfair.

It is important to realize that students will respect teachers who set reasonable guidelines and stick to them. Let students know that you are not angry with them for choosing consequences, that you still like them, and that they are responsible for their own circumstances. Communicate that to them by refusing to acknowledge excuses.

"Circle the two you like best."

We sat in the back of a second-grade classroom and watched as students practiced penmanship. By the time the activity ended, several rows of "M's" filled each child's paper. Mrs. Bonner, the teacher, then went to the front of the room for what we assumed was the conclusion of this activity. It was not.

What followed was a lesson as valuable as learning how to form letters. Mrs. Bonner said, "I'll be collecting your papers in a minute. Before I do, I want you to look them over carefully. Look at all your letters. Pick out a couple of them that you think you've done well, and draw circles around them. Circle the two you like best."

"Now look at your papers again," she continued. "Choose a couple of letters that are not your best; ones you'd do differently next time. Draw a line under those. It's important to me to see what you think about your penmanship." She gave them a minute to mark their papers. Then she collected them.

As students began the transition to another activity, we reflected on what we had just witnessed. Mrs. Bonner had given seven- and eight-year-old students an experience of self-evaluation. By doing so, she helped them develop an internal standard, practice the role of evaluator, and take control of their own learning.

In most classrooms, it is only the teacher who wields the red pencil. It is clear to the students that they are responsible for doing the assignments, but the teacher does the evaluation. When students accept this distinction, they abdicate responsibility for establishing their own standards and for making sure their work meets that criteria. They are not likely to reread or rewrite their own work.

By giving students experience with self-evaluation, you help them create mental models of their own best work. You help them develop personal standards of performance, and the skills to determine which products they consider acceptable. Once they internalize those standards and view evaluation as part of their role, students are more likely to modify their work as they go along.

Certainly, part of our role as teachers involves evaluating student work and effort. We do not suggest that you abandon that role. We do recommend that you expand it to include helping students learn how to evaluate themselves. The next few times when you are ready to ask students to turn in their papers, stop. Ask yourself if there is some way you can design a self-evaluation experience. Keep track of your efforts in a journal, and when you have ten, send us a copy. *And circle the two you like best.*

"Boys line up. Girls line up."

Mrs. Wilcox was interested in generating some lively discussion. She asked her third graders, "Who is smarter, man or woman?" To her delight came Andrea's bewildered inquiry, "Which man? Which woman?"

Andrea's questions indicate she does not yet generalize about the intelligence of men and women. At this point in her life she is looking beyond sex roles and stereotypical gender myths to the unique characteristics of individuals.

Mrs. Wilcox is pleased because she knows the dangers of sex-role stereotyping and the limiting effects it has on children of all ages. She is aware of how connectedness and intimacy can be undermined by sex-role bigotry, and she works hard to create a classroom environment where generalizations about the sexes are not encouraged. That is why she monitors her language.

Educators unintentionally use language patterns that foster male-female stereotyping. "Boys line up. Girls line up" is one example. What seems like a simple way to divide the classroom is actually the beginning of a subtle separation of the sexes. Children learn for the first time that the sexes are divided.

Children's awareness of their own sex dawns early in life. By school age they already have a strong awareness of themselves as boys or girls. When you ask them to line up by gender it requires no thought on their parts. However, if you vary the criteria, you give them something to think about.

We suggest dividing and grouping students based on criteria other than male/female.

"Anyone wearing red, line up for drinks."
"People with shoes that lace, bring your papers up."
"Anyone over 4'10" answer the odd questions. Four feet ten and under do the even ones."

These are ways to divide groups and point out similarities among children, as well as teach concepts. An imaginative teacher can integrate color identification, math concepts and thinking skills into the daily routine.

Educators use other phrases that contribute to sexual stereotyping. We recently heard a principal ask a fifth grade teacher, "I need some help with the lunchroom tables. Will you send down a couple of boys?" This alert teacher winked at her class and responded, "I'll send you four strong fifth graders right away." Two boys and two girls were selected.

Be careful when assigning jobs or requesting help with errands. Physical labor such as moving furniture or fetching the mop from the custodian can be handled by boys and girls, as can washing off tables or watering plants. Make sure your language communicates to all students that chores are genderless and that young men *and* young women are competent and capable of handling a variety of situations.

When Bill came in from recess, sweaty and covered with dirt, his teacher looked at him fondly and remarked, "Bill, you're all boy." Her statement was meant to show acceptance of young Bill's energy and activity, but she also revealed her expectation that boys act one way (actively) and girls another (passively). Not only is the statement "You're all boy" unhelpful, it is not even true. Bill is not all boy. None of us is all male or all female. Each of us has distinctive masculine and feminine characteristics. We need to recognize and develop a balance between both important parts of ourselves. The comment made by Bill's teacher undermines this effort.

A junior high school football coach recently told us about a particularly grueling practice he held. He smiled when he described the three fights that occurred. An appreciative grin and the following words summarized his attitude: "Boys will be boys."

"Boys will be boys" speaks of a double standard. It indicates that one set of behaviors is acceptable for young men, another for young women. When behaviors like hitting are viewed appropriate for one gender group, both groups are done a disservice. The girls are subjected to more rigid behavior standards without valid reasons. The boys are excused from learning valuable social skills and from developing mature problem-solving abilities.

"Act like a lady" is another phrase that is unhelpful. It is incongruent with child development theory that recognizes the boundless energy and curiosity which typifies childhood. Girls are admonished and penalized for behaving in ways that are comfortable and natural to their growth and their sense of self. When girls internalize this "act like a lady" message, they miss out on many of the experiences and opportunities afforded to their male peers. Their education suffers accordingly.

Sexist phrases such as the ones described here are limiting. They deny a child's individuality and emerging sense of self. They impose on children separate sets of stereotypical behaviors based on generalized criteria that ignore each child's uniqueness.

Listen for the words "boys and "girls" in your language patterns. When you hear yourself using them, check yourself. Be certain that the words you use show respect and support for each individual, regardless of gender.

"Different people have different needs."

"Jeremy gets to go to the library. That's not fair."
"Alice is eating in class. That's not fair."
"How come Brad and Bryan don't have to do both pages?
That's not fair!"

"That's not fair" is a common childhood complaint. It is an outgrowth of the myth that all students should be treated equally. Students and teachers who buy into the "equality myth" confuse equality with equity. In education, equity means all students have comparable opportunities to be educated. All are entitled to a consistent standard of experiences in the school environment. Equity does *not* mean that all students should be treated the same. No two students *are* the same, and there is no reasonable rationale for treating them that way. We would never deny glasses to a child with poor vision, but should we put glasses on every child? Will they be equal then? Of course not! The intent is that each child see clearly. Some need glasses. Some do not. *Different people have different needs.*

Jeremy gets to go to the library because he needs remediation in research skills. Alice is eating in class because she has no food at home. Brad and Bryan are only doing one page because they mastered ratio before it was introduced. Each case is unique and personal. Each requires that students be treated differently.

"Different people have different needs" helps your students understand that "fair" means more than everyone doing the same thing the same way at the same time. You teach them that "fair" means getting what they need for learning, when they need it. They learn that "fair" is really tolerance and respect for differences among people.

In their desire for disciplined, orderly classrooms, teachers sometimes create rules which undermine the notion that different people have different needs. "No talking," for instance, undermines learning for those students who *must* discuss a topic in order to remember it. "Stay in your seat" hurts the student who must move in order to attend to a subject. These inflexible rules breed conformity and force all children to behave in the same way regardless of needs.

96

It is true that if rules are to be effective, they must be enforced consistently. It is also true that classroom life presents us with a myriad of circumstances, personalities and situations. It is important that our rules serve us by giving us the security and support we need, as well as the flexibility to meet individual needs.

Flexible rules such as "Speak quietly" or "Listen while the teacher is speaking" allow for differences. "Honor your neighbor's wish for privacy" permits verbal exchange among those willing, yet respects the personal space and desires of those who want to be alone.

Rules are created by people to serve people. They must not be used to rationalize rigidity, because no matter what the rule, there will always be extenuating circumstances and special cases. All students have special needs.

When you use flexible rules to meet special needs, students notice. They see that behavioral expectations vary slightly in your classroom. They spot inconsistencies and may question the "fairness" of your approach. Use these situations to explain your beliefs about differences. Use these opportunities to model tolerance and compassion by using the phrase, "Different people have different needs."

"Different people have different needs" is language that encourages uniqueness, creativity, and acceptance. It discourages bigotry, elitism, and put-downs. When this phrase becomes common in your classroom, slow learners or disabled students will not be viewed as inferior, only different. Gifted youngsters will not be viewed as better, just different. There will be no stigma attached to being different, since everyone is!

People are equal only according to law. School is not about enforcing the law, but about helping children create themselves as thinking, tolerant, compassionate *individuals*. Every child really is different and deserves to have those differences accepted and respected. Every teacher has the responsibility to address those differences so children can learn maximally. When teachers seek to meet the different needs of different children, *everyone* is special, because differences are the norm. As your students develop their own unique potentials, they can be guided and served by the tolerance and wisdom of the phrase "Different people have different needs."

"Inch by inch."

Human development is an orderly growth process which consists of a series of tasks to be confronted and mastered. At the physical level we can say simply that one learns to crawl before walking and learns to walk before running. Each task involves much playful practice and experimentation. Growth is orderly, sequential, and gradual. It happens little by little, inch by inch.

Students do not always understand that human growth occurs one step at a time. They become impatient to write before their fingers can perform the task. They tackle a huge project and become frustrated by the enormity of it. They rush to complete an assignment, only to find the finished product does not meet their internal standard of perfection. They watch another student type and conclude that they will never match that skill level. These students need teachers who understand human development. They need teachers who realize that children are exactly where they are supposed to be, and that with support and encouragement, the next steps will occur naturally.

A reassuring hand on the shoulder and a gentle reminder, "Inch by inch, Chad," can help a child relax and accept his current ability level. "One step at a time, Ricky" can precede teaching the notion that large goals can be broken up into smaller ones. A warm smile and "Little by little, Caitlin" may reduce frustration.

"Inch by inch" and similar phrases tend to reduce students' stress and give them permission to enjoy learning. This style of teacher talk slows the rush to completion that dominates our product-centered schools, and puts more emphasis on the learning process. "Inch by inch" allows students to enjoy the process of creating a project. It helps them see that the creativity involved in planning and executing a clay pot is as valuable as the completed pottery.

"Inch by inch" encourages students to experiment, manipulate, and take risks. It invites them to relax, have fun, and become comfortable with their learning. They can get playful with tasks and take the time to talk about them. When students understand that learning takes place one step at a time, and that they are developing steadily in their own unique way, they enjoy the process of learning, delighting in each small step along the way. Inch by inch.

"You just lost ten minutes."

A popular penalty for misbehavior in classrooms is withholding a portion of gym or recess. The rationale is that if students are in danger of losing a part of school that they really enjoy, they will eliminate disruptive behaviors. This "discipline" method is commonly implemented when students are slow to quiet themselves (verbally and physically), and may take one of the following forms:

"There goes your gym period."
"Sounds like you really don't want recess today."
"Hey, go ahead and goof around. I don't care if you miss gym today."
"That's five minutes."
"You just lost ten minutes."

We believe that the strategy of taking away gym to produce desired behaviors is unhealthy, unskillful, and undermines important educational goals. The ends do not justify the means. In fact, the means do not even lead to the desired ends.

In one fourth-grade classroom we observed, the entire class lost ten minutes of recess because two students chose not to quiet down upon request. The school's motto was "I am in charge of me," yet in that classroom no matter how "in charge" of herself a student chose to be, one disruptive classmate could take away gym or recess. In this case, "You just lost ten minutes" is incongruent with the goal of developing self-responsible students.

Many teachers *say* they believe "gym is just as important as any other subject," yet we never see them taking away ten minutes of math or reading. Their behavior reduces the "gym as important" message to meaningless words.

Teachers who take gym away as punishment probably do not realize that physical education is crucial to intellectual development. The brain is part of a larger biological system and cannot function to capacity if the whole system is not working at top efficiency. Daily vigorous physical activity is *imperative* to learning, as is the development of gross motor coordination. A body that is awake, alive, and physically fit is more receptive to learning. When teachers take away gym and recess, they undermine their own goals of developing student intellect. Physical and intellectual learning are interdependent, so by failing to accommodate the *whole* child, teachers weaken the entire system.

The "you just lost ten minutes" strategy pits one student against another, as the majority often become disgusted with the few whose behavior causes them problems. While some educators espouse this method of negative peer pressure, we believe it is harmful and self-defeating. It is harmful, because disruptive students are often encouraged by negative attention from the peer group. They are unskillful at making friends and lack social skills. Consequently, they settle for any kind of attention, good or bad, they can solicit from their classmates. The teacher who uses this method of discipline, actually discourages helpful social behaviors and friendships. Instead of helping these special-needs students, they help to defeat them. The method is self-defeating because cooperation is actively discouraged. There can be no collaborative atmosphere of unity and belonging if we pit students against one another through the use of negative peer pressure.

It is our belief that the "you just lost ten minutes" method of classroom control does not work. Students who are disruptive have problems that are not dealt with when teachers mete out this style of punishment. These students need listening, problem solving, positive attention, understanding and counseling. They need a chance to "blow off steam," with vigorous physical exercise. They need constructive ways to *e*rupt so they do not need so much to *dis*rupt. Taking gym away from these children does not work because it is like capping a volcano. There may be an explosion.

Students lose respect for the teacher as they recognize and resent the unfairness and incongruence of this method of control. As with all efforts to control children, it demonstrates a basic lack of faith in their abilities to control themselves. It is swift, arbitrary *punishment*, not discipline, that has nothing to do with cause and effect, or consequences for one's own actions. Children become disillusioned with the educational system when they see that these respected adults behave inconsistently with what they say they believe. Because children learn best when there is an emotional connection and respect for the teacher, this disillusionment has a damaging effect on their learning.

Effective teachers encourage cooperation and unity by guiding and encouraging students. They work on congruence between their actions and their words, and they shun arbitrary punishment. They understand the delicate balance between the physical and the intellectual, and do not take away what children need. Effective teachers value the learning and development of the whole child.

"Act your age."

Patty could not seem to make up her mind what color of construction paper she wanted for her art project. She took orange, then changed to blue, and finally decided on red. Then, when all the papers were passed out, she noticed that Candy had green and she was sure *she* wanted that color. The teacher relented, exchanging red for green, and Patty pouted because she was not first for green. She began to cry. In exasperation, Patty's teacher chided, "Act your age!"

Patty actually *was* acting her age. Developmental characteristics of six-year-olds include ambivalence, stubbornness, and frequent tears. Patty is being punished for acting like a six-year-old. She can hardly miss the irritation and rejection in her teacher's words. Her *self* is being attacked. By not accepting the child that Patty actually is, by struggling against understandable, *normal* six-year-old behavior, the teacher is undermining the child's self-esteem and is creating needless stress for herself.

Teachers who understand human growth and the behavioral characteristics of their students are less likely to view age-appropriate behavior as misbehavior. When teachers understand the developmental reasons behind the forgetfulness of seven-year-olds or the put-downs of preadolescents, they will be more accepting of students and less likely to use this unhelpful phrase. It will then be possible to approach students' behaviors from a calm and accepting stance. The teacher will feel less provoked and stressed, and more able to teach.

"Act your age" hints that the child's behavior is somehow unacceptable. Yet it is too general and vague to teach the student which behaviors *are* appropriate. If teachers want certain student behaviors to manifest and others to be eliminated, they must accept the child where he or she is at that moment, while suggesting and encouraging specific behavioral alternatives.

"Joellen, next time wait for your turn. You'll usually get one" helps Joellen understand exactly what you want. "Patty, do eenie-meenie to help you decide" is language that gives Patty an option to consider. "Dave, someone may get hurt if you run in this crowd" teaches the reason behind the rule of walking in the lunchroom.

"Act your age" does not instruct or help the child understand what behaviors are expected. Instead, it communicates disrespect and misunderstanding. If you wish to make your language congruent with your experience, education and desire to nurture children, eliminate "act your age" from your teacher talk.

"Don't you talk to me like that!"

Students often challenge adults with comments like "I don't have to," "What makes you think you're so smart?" or "You can't make me." They use their words as bait in an attempt to distract our attention from the real issue and hook us into a power struggle.

If you hear yourself respond, "Don't you talk to me like that!" be assured you have swallowed the hook. You are caught and the struggle is on.

"Don't you talk to me like that!" indicates you have interpreted the student's words as attack. Perceiving attack, you become defensive. Defensiveness prevents you from accurately hearing the real content of the student's message. As you defend yourself, the conflict escalates.

It is possible to respond effectively to antagonistic statements by remembering that angry students feel attacked and afraid. Their words are unskillful cries for help. We suggest that you focus on the feelings of the student involved. Temporarily ignore the verbal content of his message and speak to his feelings rather than his words. "You must be furious to talk like that. Let's talk about it when you are less upset" responds to the child's feelings and lets him know that you are taking him seriously. "I hear your anger and I'd like you to express it in different words" acknowledges the strong emotion. It tells the student that you dislike their choice of words, and you care about their pain. "You're really upset. It's not like you to talk like that" shifts the emphasis from *what* the student said to the emotion beneath it.

Recently we witnessed a secondary science teacher initiate a discussion about tardiness with one late student. "Oh, lighten up!" the student responded with a roll of her eyes. This teacher responded with skill and understanding. He analyzed the outburst as an attempt to divert attention from the real problem. "Becky, I sense your frustration and can see your tardiness is not as big a concern to you as it is to me. I want to discuss it further. Meet me after class," he told her. Comfortable in his teaching stance, he ignored further grumbling by the student and continued with his lesson.

This teacher responded to the student's feelings with professionalism instead of emotionalism. He refused to speak from a defensive or counter-attacking position, and did not get "hooked." He was not distracted by the student's unskillful, even hostile way of expressing herself and was able to empower her while retaining his own sense of personal power. Later, when the student calmed down he would deal specifically with the issue of tardiness.

Centering your response on students' feelings rather than their rebellious choice of words helps you to acknowledge their feelings without reacting defensively. It lets them know you heard them at a deeper level. It keeps you in control and keeps their dignity intact.

"I don't like what I just heard.
If you're angry, tell me another way."

Sometimes student name-calling is directed at teachers. It may take a gentle form of attack such as "You're clumsy." It could be sent wrapped in judgment like "That's stupid." Or it might even take on a sarcastic edge, "You gotta be kidding!" Whatever form it takes, teacher skill is necessary to deal with it effectively. A skillful response we suggest is "I don't like what I just heard. If you're angry, tell me another way." This phrase communicates respect for yourself and respect for the child.

When you share this key phrase with students you are really saying, "I have too much respect for myself to be talked to this way. Please share your thoughts and feelings in a way that honors me as a person." This form of communication also shows respect for the child. It announces "I think your feelings are important. You have a right to express them here. I will listen to you and consider your feedback. Please tell me in a way that gives me useful information."

When you use this form of teacher talk with children, you are modeling self-respect in action. You are not only teaching them how you want to be treated, you are showing them a way to communicate how *they* wish to be treated.

108

"What did you really want to tell her?"

"I think you're selfish."
"I hate you!"
"You stupid jerk."

Comments like the ones listed above are delivered by students to students. It often represents their best effort, under stress, to communicate with a classmate. The communication is unhelpful, because it escalates the conflict.

Teachers who notice students using this non-productive style of communication are faced with alternatives. They can launch into tirades on the evils of name-calling. They can use these opportunities to demonstrate problem solving, or they can explain to students the class policy on put-downs.

"What did you really want to tell her?" is our suggested alternative. It asks the child uttering the put-down to stop and think. It forces her to become conscious, and challenges her to get in touch with what it is she really wants.

Many students are not tuned in to the responsibility they have to get things the way they want them. Hence, they take the stance that the other person is responsible and choose name-calling in an effort to change their classmate. They give up their power by concentrating on the half of the interaction over which they have the least control.

When students are guided to discover and articulate their wants, "I don't like it when you put your foot on the desk," they have re-claimed their personal power. They have done so by choosing to focus on the responsibility *they* have to get things the way they want them.

Another drawback associated with name-calling is that it lets the other person off the hook. If students do not give clear, descriptive information on how they are reacting to the behavior of their peers, they protect their peers from having to look at how the behavior impacts others. When students call names, they give others a built-in excuse to get angry back. The issue now becomes the name-calling rather than the precipitating behavior.

"What did you really want to tell her?" reminds students to determine what they want and examine their language patterns to see if the two are congruent. Other ways to communicate the same message are listed below:

"If you call her a name, she won't know why you're upset."
"What would you like her to do differently next time?"
"With all those names, how did she know what you wanted?"

Each is a variation of the "What did you really want to tell her?" theme. Each is a way to help students focus on their own role in the interaction. Each helps students become more self-responsible.

"Stop daydreaming."

On the first day of the new school year, a teacher was reviewing class rules with her first graders. She instructed the children that they must be *doing* something at all times of the school day. One six-year-old raised her hand and asked, "What about thinking? Is thinking doing something?" Without hesitation, the teacher answered, "No. Thinking doesn't count."

Although most teachers probably find this incident shocking, it is a true story that indicates how little thinking is valued in schools. Forty years after Bloom and his colleagues published the hierarchy of thinking, many textbooks do not pose questions beyond the comprehension level. True/false and multiple choice tests dominate, and product is valued far more than process. The Scholastic Aptitude Test (SAT) clearly emphasizes recall of information. The majority of intellectual tasks in schools are simply memorization, the lowest level of thought in the hierarchy. Although few educators would quarrel with the notion that thinking is a legitimate school activity, it is not supported or encouraged in schools across the country. Thinking is quiet and unobservable. Therefore, students engaged in thinking may appear to be doing nothing. Doing nothing is unacceptable in schools, because it lowers the amount of time on task. Since time spent on task helps students complete assignments and memorize information, that time is highly valued by educators. Thinking, if misinterpreted as doing nothing, is not allowed.

Teachers assume that idle students indicate idle minds. "Stop daydreaming," we tell our students when it appears they are not *doing* something. They could be deep in thought, planning, projecting, analyzing, evaluating, or rehearsing. Yet our need for "on task" behaviors predominates and "Stop daydreaming" becomes the signal that ends their thinking.

Recent research on successful, gifted women shows that one thing these successful people had in common was a great deal of time alone when they were children; time to think, to daydream. Another study points out that the only discernible difference in the upbringing of geniuses and other bright children was that the families in which genius was nurtured valued time alone. They accepted and encouraged fantasy and daydreams.

We believe that daydreaming *is* thinking. It is thinking at its best, because it is visionary. World leaders, corporate magnates, inventors, composers, artists, and authors are all creative thinkers. Without dreams, fantasies, and visions, these great men and women would have stuck to "time on task" and never have the thoughts that create their greatness.

We suggest that teachers consider incorporating a "Thinking Time" into their daily schedule. This ten or fifteen minutes of class time can take the form of serious academic thought or of mind play. Both are valuable. The mind at play functions at a highly sophisticated level as it tries out various possibilities and relates school learning to its real world. Thinking time is a personal, silent time of planning, fantasizing, or quiet introspection. Often students are too busy "doing" in school to have time to think about *what* they are doing or *how* or *why*. A short daily period of thinking, followed by class discussion that helps students process, or think about their thinking, will help solve this problem and will show students that as teachers we value and support thinking. The payoffs will be great in all subjects, as minds develop along with academic skills. As educators we show children, with our actions and words, that thinking does count by announcing daily, "It's thinking time."

"Always do your best."

"Always do your best."
"Anything worth doing is worth doing well."
"Make your best better."

The phrases above have been spoken over public address systems and placed on banners in schools throughout the country. Some are school mottos. Others have appeared on letterheads. They are intended to communicate a standard of excellence to students.

"Do your best" and similar phrases seem at first glance to fit our goals of creating high expectations and of encouraging students to strive for excellence. Always doing one's best, however, is impossible. Striving to always do one's best is undesirable. These phrases may conflict with what we really want to communicate to our students.

In our daily lives, much of what we do is automatic. We wake up, turn off the alarm clock, brush our teeth. We do those things to get them done. There is no goal of excellence. It is not important to do our best.

Some days we might dress for an important meeting or job interview. On those occasions we want to look our "best." Other days we know we are going to clean the house and do jigsaw puzzles with the kids, so we can comfortably slip into sweats. Our best dress is unimportant.

Students may need to give their best for an exam or a special project, but do they really need to do their best when practice, experimentation, or completion of a first draft are the goals? How about when students are authoring a short story for the first time? Do we really want them to be focusing on doing their best, or would it be more helpful if they concentrated on getting their thoughts on paper? Is it helpful to ask a student who has never attempted cursive writing to do her best on a practice sheet or is it more important that she be comfortable enough to experiment with the new skill? Perhaps doing their best is best saved for more appropriate times.

What is our best, anyway? Does anyone ever do their best? Who decides what is a student's best? How does one person know the exact level of another person's potential?

Our daughter came home distraught from school one day. The annual year-end awards assembly was approaching. The students had been advised that special awards would be given to "good students." Her teacher informed them, "If you did your best this year, you have nothing to worry about." Allison was furious. "How does *she* know if I did my best?" she fumed. "What if somebody got all 'D's' and it *was* their best? What if somebody got all 'A's' and it *wasn't* their best? If I don't get an award, everyone will think I didn't do my best!" Her anguish was intense.

In the end, all students in Allison's class got the award. Did they all do their best? Did any really do their best? What about those students who know they did not do their best? Are they left to feel unworthy of an award they received, or do they sense the phoniness of the "do your best" philosophy and chalk it up as another incongruent adult communication?

One problem with "Always do your best" is that it can manifest as stress in high achievers. Highly motivated learners may have developed a perfectionist mentality that pushes them to do their best. They live in a state of anxiety wondering, "Will my best be good enough?" Sadly, it never is enough, because they are likely to believe that one can always "make the best better." The focus of these young lives is on creating "best" outcomes. When every project in every area of their lives must be their best, these students court burnout.

Some youngsters who are constantly badgered to do their best, do *not* become perfectionists. Instead, they resign themselves to inferior schoolwork and feelings of inadequacy. Others choose enjoyment of the learning process over perfectionism, then suffer guilt because they are not doing their "best."

When we say, "Do your best," we really mean "This is important." When we tell students, "Make your best better," we mean "I'd like you to treat this assignment with extreme seriousness."

It is important that we eliminate platitudes like "Do your best" from our vocabulary. Students are likely to respond positively when we say what we really mean, because we provide them with information that is direct and meaningful. If this is an important test, let them know. If this typing lesson is a timed skill test, give them the facts. Vary your language. Save "Do your best" for those rare times when it is crucial that students summon their energy and motivation to create their own brand of excellence. Save "Do your best" for those times when you really mean it.

"My patience is running out."

Patience is thought to be a characteristic of good teachers, parents, even saints. It has long been considered a virtue. "She has the patience of Job." "She's so patient with those little children." "Oh, I admire your patience!" We challenge the traditional point of view that patience is desirable, and encourage all teachers to consider their use of this word.

One dictionary defines patient as *"bearing pains or trials calmly or without complaints; manifesting forbearance under provocation or strain; steadfast despite opposition, difficulty, or adversity."* Another describes patient as *"capable of bearing affliction with calmness."*

Is this really what we want from teachers? Do we want them to "bear pains calmly?" Do we want educators to view children as the opposition, and students as adversaries? We do not think so. We believe that instead of "manifesting forbearance" in patience, teachers need *understanding.*

The teacher who understands the developmental capabilities of the students he teaches does not need to "bear pains calmly." He will accept behaviors that are developmentally appropriate and will not see the child as an adversary. The child will be viewed as innately good, though inexperienced. Teachers who understand their students will see themselves as partners in learning and will not view the child as "opposition." This adult will approach the learning situation and the child as a pleasure rather than an adversary, a trial, or a difficulty.

An effective teacher may not possess a great deal of patience, but will understand children's needs and motivations. His virtue is not patience, because the grit-your-teeth-and-bear-it teacher cannot be truly effective. His virtue is the behavior that flows from understanding that children need teachers as guides and role models.

When you hear yourself say, "My patience is wearing thin; I'm getting impatient; my patience is running out," remind yourself that if you can *understand*, patience will be unnecessary. Use these words as a signal to question yourself. Ask, "What is it here that I don't understand?" Remind yourself, "I'm not understanding this situation." Tell yourself, "I don't understand this behavior." This will help you to consider other points of view. Pausing to remind yourself that patience indicates a lack of understanding will help you to move out of an emotional reaction and into an effective teaching stance.

While the patient teacher is likely to see himself as a martyr, struggling through days of adversity imposed by the children, the understanding teacher will celebrate *with* them the process of growth and development. As understanding teachers welcome student behaviors that patient teachers find irritating, enthusiasm and joy will result for all.

"Put your baseball cards away. It's time for math."

She bought her first pack of baseball cards at age five. By the time she was six, she had learned to spread them on the floor, sorting by number, figuring out which ones were missing. She called it playing. We call it ordering numerals.

During the next two years, she counted baseball cards, sorted them by team, position, league, and personal preference, and began an interest in statistics. She learned to read positions, cities, and names of players. She discovered abbreviations, made comparisons and computed players' ages. In third grade her teacher told her, "Put your baseball cards away.

"Put your baseball cards away. It's time for math" is a statement that is symbolic of a major problem in our schools. This phrase emphasizes the importance of curriculum, and signifies disregard for child-centered education.

The "put your baseball cards away" message informs students that schedules and lesson plans are valued more than their own interests. They learn that the teacher's interest is in covering material and that the teacher's loyalty is to the curriculum.

When students' interests are not as important as "the material," they fail to see the connection between their real lives and what they are asked to learn. They may be unmotivated, because they do not understand why schoolwork is necessary.

Child-centered teachers understand that the most valuable education draws from the child's own experience. They realize that math is not just a subject in a book, but also a part of our everyday lives. They use real life experiences to teach it.

In a child-centered classroom, children come first and the agenda follows. Since these teachers are well-informed on child development theory and appropriate age-level content objectives, they do not have to rely on textbook companies and ditto sheet packets to make curriculum decisions for them. They recognize that they are constantly presented with the material necessary to teach math, writing, spelling, and self-responsibility. They cover content by using the real-life issues and interests of their students, finding opportunities to teach in butterflies, Barbie dolls, rocks, *and* baseball cards.

"Ask three before me."

Twenty-eight students work quietly on a page of math problems. Although a thorough explanation preceded the individual practice portion of this lesson, several students are confused. Hands fill the air as students signal for help. The teacher moves around the room as quickly as possible, offering explanations and encouragement, but students grow impatient from waiting. Both the teacher and the students are frustrated with the time wasted.

"Ask three before me" is a phrase that, if used consistently and backed up with appropriate teacher action, will eliminate scenes like the one above. The underlying messages of this phrase are "The teacher is *not* the source of all knowledge here" and "We are expected to learn *interdependently*."

The "ask three" pattern releases the teacher from the sole responsibility for helping. Students are encouraged to turn to each other for help *before* approaching the teacher. Many questions are handled in this manner and students are freed to move ahead with their practice. The teacher has made himself dispensable now, and is able to concentrate on students whose questions require a more detailed explanation.

The "ask three before me" philosophy also helps students see themselves and each other as valuable resources. They see each other as able, capable and willing to assist. In addition, they learn how to solicit and offer assistance, becoming learning enablers as well as learners. They actively experience the concepts of independence, interdependence and collaboration. When students rely on each other regularly, connectedness grows, trust increases and relationships are strengthened.

The next time a student approaches with a request for help, make yourself dispensable. Suggest that the student, "Ask three before me."

"Someone in your group knows."

Whether you divide students into groups for social studies, use lab teams in your science program, or design lessons around the cooperative learning model, this phrase can be a useful tool. It communicates to students your expectations that group members are responsible to each other, that you believe the group contains the resources necessary to solve the problem at hand, and that they are to look *inside* the group for answers and ideas.

Two minutes after you have given instructions on items to include during group presentations, Bill asks, "Do we have to include all seven areas?" Your response? "Someone in your group knows."

Halfway into work time Bonita wonders aloud, "Do we all sign our names on these like last time?" The response remains consistent. "Someone in your group knows."

As the allotted time winds down, an excited group member blurts out, "What do we do when we're finished?" Instantly from within the same group comes the reply, "I'm in your group. I know."

Student responses like the one above help make teaching rewarding as well as fun, and they do not happen by accident. They occur when teachers set out with intentionality to behave as interactionists rather than interventionists.

Interventionists believe it is their job to intervene in groups. When they see groups struggling, they go over and solve the problem. When asked a question, they give the answer. They communicate through their words and actions that groups do not work very well unless teachers straighten them out.

Interactionists believe their job is to turn problems back to the group. When groups struggle, they ask the groups to examine the struggle. When asked a question, they reflect it back to the group for an answer. They communicate through their words and actions that, with a minimum of teacher interaction, groups will work well and straighten themselves out.

Before group work begins, announce what role you will play. Tell students you believe each group has the resources and the capacity to complete the task. Let them know what you will do if a group struggles or asks for assistance. Then follow through. Do what you said you would do, and remember to use the phrase "Someone in your group knows."

"Is that a group question?"

Sometimes nobody in the group can answer one member's question. Students query each other and generate no satisfactory responses. At this point it is helpful for the teacher to provide the answer from within the structure of the interactionist role.

Interactionists encourage students to rely on each other. They want each group to trust that they possess the resources necessary to work productively and independently. Before group work begins, interactionist teachers give clear directions that include a thorough explanation of the teacher's role during work time. They share with students their belief that groups contain enough resources to work effectively. They tell the class that their initial reaction to questions will be "Someone in your group knows." If no one in the group can answer, together students may formulate a group question.

A group question is any question that has been discussed in the group, is understood by every group member, and cannot be answered satisfactorily by anyone within the group. When there is a group question, students raise their hands and the teacher continues in the interactionist role. The teacher approaches the group and asks, "Is this a group question?" If all agree that it is, the teacher randomly chooses one group member to ask the question. The student who initiates the question, is not the one who is asked to articulate it. If the spokesperson can articulate the question, it is answered by the teacher. If the spokesperson cannot repeat the question, then the guidelines for a group question have not been met. The teacher turns it back to the group for further consideration.

When teachers function consistently as interactionists, it is only a short time before students increasingly settle problems within the group, without teacher assistance. This is a time for celebration. Your belief that students can rely on and assist one another, as well as your insistence that they do so, have paid off.

"Say you're sorry."

When we say, "Tell him you're sorry," the message is "Forget what you would really like to say. Hold back your anger. Choke off your frustration. Push down all your real feelings and pretend they don't exist." When we ask angry students to apologize, we do them a disservice by teaching them to deny their feelings. It is unhealthy for students to believe that some feelings are better than others, that "negative" feelings should not be expressed or felt, and that pretending is more important than expressing authentic feelings. Instead we must allow our students to experience their feelings and to express them in responsible ways that lead to the resolution of problems and to more comfortable feelings.

Sometimes "Tell him you're sorry" gives students an easy out. It is a simple penance which excuses them from considering a change in their behavior. They do not have to create plans for more appropriate action or think about how to behave differently in the future. They do not have to think at all. They only have to say, "I'm sorry."

If a student is not sorry, do not coerce her into pretending differently. Use your skills to help that student get in touch with her real feelings and communicate them in descriptive, nonjudgmental language. Say, "Tell him you are angry because when he called you stupid it felt like a put-down," or "Let Bob know you're frustrated at the amount of time he's taking at the art center."

If a student *is* sorry, certainly she can be encouraged to say so. This can be a cleansing release of guilt that allows the student to get on with her day. When real regret exists, help students learn from their mistakes. Teach your students to express what they have learned from their behavior and what they are going to do differently next time. This is enough. Students do *not* have to feel remorse, regret or self-criticism to learn from mistakes.

"I learned that you don't like me cutting in front of you in line and it's my intention not to do that again" leaves the student feeling more powerful and self-responsible than "I'm sorry I did it. I apologize. Please forgive me."

"I learned you don't like my copying off your paper" leaves the child with greater self-esteem than "I apologize for copying your answer. I'm sorry."

"I'm sorry" language leaves the child focusing on wrong-doing, feeling small, and hoping to be forgiven. It is a way of speaking that lowers self-esteem, personal power and confidence. The goal-directed "I learned and I intend" style helps them focus on learning and positive intention.

It is less important to say we are sorry than to behave as if it is so. When we drop the "Tell him you're sorry" phrase from our language patterns, we help our students concentrate on learning. We teach them the valuable lesson that to be sorry means to behave differently.

"I understand just how you feel."

"I understand just how you feel" is an effort to empathize with students. Teachers use it to reassure students that they, too, have experienced fear, doubt, anger, or frustration. They want to communicate "I know what that's like for you. I've been there, too. I understand."

Nobody can understand exactly how another person feels. No two people, their experiences, or their perceptions of those experiences are ever the same. We are all different and so is our experience of life.

When children are experiencing strong emotion, a part of them wants to believe that no one else has ever felt that way. They want to believe that nobody has ever been this much in love or felt pain so excruciating. They want to be taken seriously for the uniqueness of their experience.

On the other hand, children want to know that their feelings are normal. They want reassurance that they will not be overwhelmed by their feelings, that others have survived those same emotions.

Because of this paradox ("nobody has every felt this way and everybody has felt this way"), the teacher is never sure if the words "I understand just how you feel" will be met with relief or resentment. We suggest that you drop this phrase from your teacher talk, and instead *demonstrate* that you understand with active listening.

Active Listening is the best way we know to demonstrate understanding when a student is experiencing strong emotion. In order to perform this skill effectively, you must first *be quiet and listen.* Attend with your body. Give the student strong eye contact, open body posture, and get down on their level, physically. Do not interrupt their narrative. When the child stops talking, paraphrase what you heard and saw. State the feeling and a possible reason:

"You feel _____ because _____."

If Robert tells you he is mad because girls have been chasing and teasing him at recess, *do not presume* you understand. Use a reflective response to check out the accuracy of your understanding. Do not use Robert's exact words. Demonstrate your understanding by paraphrasing what he said. Say, "You sound angry because girls are getting after you" or you might say, "The girls are razzing you and you're upset."

If your words accurately reflect Robert's feelings, he will acknowledge that and feel understood. He is likely to continue his dialogue, blowing off steam and giving you more information. Again, use active listening skills by altering his words as you reflect back his feelings and concerns. *Remember, you are listening. This is not a time to give advice or soothe feelings. Just listen actively.*

If your initial paraphrase is inaccurate, Robert can correct the misconception by restating or embellishing his original comments. Either way you arrive at a position of understanding.

When Teresa shares her reaction to being cut from the softball team, refrain from saying, "I know what that's like," even though you have vivid memories of being dropped from the Junior Varsity basketball squad. Instead, reflect her feelings and concerns in your own words. "You feel cheated because you didn't get a chance to really show your skill." It is unnecessary to give advice to tell her she should not feel bad, or to help her solve her problems. All you need to do is listen skillfully. Teresa is comforted and encouraged, simply because she feels understood.

Reflective listening is an act of respect. It informs students "I don't know exactly how you feel, but I'm ready to listen and I want to understand. I'm willing to check it out and see if I got it right. You are worth this time and energy." As you practice, your active listening skills will improve. You will notice how much students appreciate your efforts, how they are comforted when they believe that another person really does understand their feelings and concerns. The teacher-student relationship and the feelings of connectedness will grow, as will the number of students who come to you for listening. Your satisfaction will increase as you improve your ability to reassure distraught students with active listening.

"Make a picture in your mind."

Quiet yourself for a moment. Relax and breathe deeply. Make a picture in your mind of yourself using helpful, new language patterns with your students. See yourself having fun with the examples presented in this book. Notice your enthusiasm as you play with this style of language. Watch as your students react positively. See them responding in ways that indicate increased self-responsibility and feelings of self-worth. Notice how they cooperate with one another and behave interdependently. Watch as their behaviors indicate an increasing sense of personal power and self-esteem.

Now picture yourself at the end of the day. See yourself relaxed, satisfied, fulfilled. Notice how pleased you are with yourself, your emerging language patterns, and the results you are getting. Enjoy the pictures for a few moments. Then, read on.

The activity above is called positive picturing or mental rehearsal. It is the use of the imagination to picture the positive process and outcome of an upcoming activity. Using the technique as it is described above will help you achieve your new language goals.

One element significantly related to achievement is the ability to visualize desired outcomes. Chances are, if you are not able to imagine yourself behaving in a certain way, you will not be able to behave that way. If you cannot see yourself using this style of language, you may not use it. By creating a positive picture in your mind, you increase the odds for success.

Positive picturing is a strategy you can use with students at any grade level. Young children can make a picture in their minds of finding just the right book on their excursion to the library. Before your high school students type a business letter, help them to visualize it in their minds. Help them to see in their mind the heading, greeting, body, and appropriate closing. Prior to choosing partners, ask students to picture themselves pairing with someone they do not often choose. At the end of class, ask them to visualize arriving on time the next day, with a notebook, text, and pencils.

"Make a picture in your mind" helps clarify your expectations to students. Use this language to specify the behaviors and levels of performance you desire. We know one teacher who uses this strategy prior to every assembly. *"Children,"* she begins, *"close your eyes gently and relax. Make a picture in your mind of our class walking quietly into the gym, single file, arms at our sides. Notice one of your friends calling out to you. You smile and nod your head silently. Look! Every member of the class has taken their seat quickly and watches the front. Feel your pride and sense of maturity as you are quietly unaffected by those around you."*

Another teacher we observed, used mental rehearsal to introduce an activity. It allowed students to experience the situation mentally before they attempted it physically. *"Today we will be painting at the easel for the first time. Close your eyes and see yourself approach the easel. Stop now and push up your sleeves. Take a paint shirt from the hook and put it on backwards. See? The buttons are on the back. Ask a friend to fasten the top button for you. Who did you ask? See them in your mind. Now you are ready to paint. Choose a color, pick up a brush and gently wipe it on the side of the cup. See? Now there are very few drips while you paint. Watch yourself place the brush back into the color that matches. That way the colors won't get mixed in the cups. Notice how you remember to mix the colors on your paper. Stroke, dab, swirl. Enjoy creating your picture.*

Okay, now your painting is done. Oh, you like it so much that you decide to leave it right on the easel to dry so it won't get messed up. See yourself take the sponge out of the bucket and squeeze the water out. You wipe up all the paint drips off the floor without leaving any puddles! Now you wash your hands and dry them. Remove the paint shirt and replace it on the hook. Stand back and admire your art work. Feel how responsible and capable you are!"

Does visualizing the process of using the easel insure that colors will not get mixed? Does it eliminate drips on paintings, messes on floors, and confusion at the easel? Of course not. It will, however, increase your chances of getting what you want more of the time.

Positive picturing will help you influence how your students see themselves, and consequently, how they perform. Students who see themselves as leaders act like leaders. Students who see themselves as readers act like readers.

Martin saw himself as a klutz and a failure at gym time. His skill level did not match that of his peers and he did not feel that his contributions to the team effort were helpful. Martin's eighth-grade physical education instructor was skilled in positive picturing, knew its benefits, and designed an activity to improve the situation. Mrs. Millar had all students close their eyes and unwind. She then led them through a visualization that highlighted effort rather than skill. She had them imagine the value of organizing, settling disputes, and accepting wins as well as losses with grace and humility. The result of this activity was that many of the students changed their perception of the "klutzy" Martin. Martin recognized himself in the scenario, and even though his physical education skills did not immediately improve, he was able to acknowledge his attributes and improve his own self-perception.

Positive picturing will help your students reach their goals. Students can visualize themselves making the basketball team, writing in cursive, or reading fluently. They can see themselves passing the test, finishing the science project, or handing in the term paper. The ability to visualize a desire is one big step towards attaining it. Repetitive positive picturing empowers students by teaching them that they can direct their own thoughts and imagination toward achieving a desired result.

When you ask a student to make a picture in his mind, you engage his right brain. That is the part of the brain that thinks holistically and is responsible for imagination and intuition. Since most school instruction involves the logical, linear, left brain, positive picturing helps create a balance. When the student involves the whole brain, learning increases and success multiplies.

Once again, quiet yourself for a moment. Relax and breathe deeply. Make a picture in your mind of yourself using positive picturing with your students. Rehearse mentally, seeing yourself as successful. Feel the feelings associated with success. Enjoy your excitement as well as theirs. Review the entire scene in your mind as you experience satisfaction. Know that this mental rehearsal is moving you closer to using this strategy effectively with your students. Expect that you will be skilled in telling students "Make a picture in your mind."

"Touch each other gently."

Some researchers believe that a minimum of eight hugs each day are necessary to maintain mental health. Others believe that if people would learn to touch one another, conflict among people and nations would be greatly reduced. It is a well-documented fact that the very young and the very old may die from a lack of physical touch.

Our society suffers from a debilitating condition called "skin hunger." It undermines our physical well-being, and our mental health and happiness. Because of this, it is crucial that teachers teach children to touch each other in supportive and appropriate ways. We must model gentle, nurturing touching, provide a supportive environment, and encourage touch with such phrases as "Touch each other gently."

Children touch and manipulate their environment in order to grow. They touch to bond and connect with other people. Encouraging children to "touch each other gently" is encouraging them to learn and grow. It communicates to them that appropriate touching is accepted and appreciated in your classroom.

"Touch each other gently" is an inviting, supportive alternative to the phrase "Keep your hands to yourself." It says what you *really* mean and puts a positive picture of what you really want in children's minds.

When a kindergartner pushes another child out of line, remind her, "Touch each other gently."

When third graders are poking each other in the lunch line, advise, "Touch each other gently."

When sixth graders say "I like you" by punching each other in the stomach, insist, "Touch each other gently."

Unfortunately, most children are not very skillful at soliciting the kind of touch that they want and need. They satisfy their hunger with pokes and swats at peers, necking and petting with teenage loves, even pre-adolescent sex. They have learned about touching from violent and sexually-oriented television and movies, from spankings, and from societal prejudice against people touching people. Throughout the school years teachers have admonished, "Keep your hands to yourselves."

Please begin now to teach students that touching is important and acceptable. Teach them by modeling appropriate touch, by creating opportunities for students to encourage each other and to come in close contact, and by implementing the phrase "Touch each other gently."

IN CONCLUSION

Despite the truism, talk is *not* cheap. It is expensive. Every time you talk to students, you send two messages: the message of your words and the silent underlying message.

The phrases and philosophies contained in this book can be powerful tools to enhance your teaching effectiveness. One word of caution, however. Words are only one of the communications to which students respond. Students are very sensitive to tone, intonation, body language, and intent. *Any* verbalizations can be rendered ineffective or harmful if the teacher's demeanor does not match the message. These phrases will work for you and for your students only when spoken from an attitude of caring and respect.

The recommended Teacher Talk are valuable and effective, *and* they are not magical. No single utterance or verbalization will transform student behavior, attitude, or achievement. Rather, the phrases will assist you in altering the pattern and style of your communications with students, so that with repeated use, you will create a classroom atmosphere where students will flourish.

If you wish to change the way you talk to students, begin today to listen to your language. Tape yourself. Monitor your words. What are you really saying to students?

Review the phrases in this book. Choose a few that seem to fit with your philosophy, your teaching style, your circumstances.

Which phrases should you attempt?
"You decide."
Not sure you *can* adopt these phrases successfully?
"Act as if."
If you fall back into old patterns?
"Next time say it differently."

Go back to your classroom, take a risk, and remember to touch your students gently.

BIBLIOGRAPHY

Arent, Ruth. Stress and Your Child. Englewood Cliffs, NJ: Prentice-Hall, Inc., 1984.

Bloom, Benjamin. All Our Children Learning. NY: McGraw-Hill, 1981.

Borba, Michele and Craig. Self-Esteem: A Classroom Affair. Minneapolis, MN: Winston Press, 1982.

Briggs, Dorothy. Celebrate Yourself. Garden City, NY: Doubleday & Co., 1977.

Canfield, Jack and Harold Wells. 100 Ways to Enhance Self-Concept in the Classroom. Englewood Cliffs, NJ: Prentice-Hall, Inc., 1976.

Carse, James P. Finite and Infinite Games. Ballantine Books, 1986.

Cazden, Courtney B. Language in Early Childhood Education. National Association for the Education for Young Children, 1987.

Cherry, Clare. Parents Please Don't Sit On Your Kids. Pitman Learning Inc., 1985.

Clemes, Harris and Reynold Bean. How To Discipline Children Without Feeling Guilty. Enirch, 1980.

Clemes, Harris and Reynold Bean. How To Raise Children's Self-Esteem. Sunnyvale, CA: Enrich Div., 1980.

Clemes, Harris and Reynold Bean. How To Teach Children Responsibility. Sunnyvale, CA: Enrich Div., 1980.

Coloroso, Barbara. Discipline: Kids Are Worth It. Media for Kids, 222 Juniper Court, Boulder, CO 80302.

Crary, Elizabeth. Kids Can Cooperate. Washington Parenting Press, 1984.

Dyer, Wayne. Gifts from Eykis. New York, NY: Simon and Schuster, 1983.

Dyer, Wayne. The Sky's the Limit. NY: Simon & Schuster, 1980.

Dyer, Wayne. What Do You Really Want for Your Child? Morrow, 1985.

Elkind, David. The Hurried Child. Addison-Wesley Publishing Company, 1981.

Faber, Adele and Elaine Mazlish. How to Talk So Kids Will Listen and Listen So Kids Will Talk. New York, NY: Rawson, Wade Publishers, Inc., 1980.

Fettig, Art. The Three Robots. Battle Creek, MI: Growth Unlimited, 1981.

Fettig, Art. _The Three Robots Discover Their Pos-abilities_. Battle Creek, MI: Growth Unlimited, 1984.

Fettig, Art. _The Three Robots and the Sandstorm_. Battle Creek, MI: Growth Unlimited, 1983.

Ginott, Haim. _Teacher and Child_. New York, NY: The Macmillan Company, 1972.

Glasser, William. _Control Theory in the Classroom_. New York, NY: Harper & Row Publishers, 1986.

Glasser, William. _Take Effective Control of Your Life_. New York, NY: Harper & Row Publishers, 1984.

Gordon, Thomas. _Teacher Effectiveness Training_. New York, NY: Peter H. Wyden, 1975.

Graham, Terry Lynne; Juliano, Rose A.; Knight, Michael E.; Miksza, Susan Robichaud; and Tonnies, Pamela G. _Teaching Children to Love Themselves_. Prentice-Hall Inc., 1982.

Hendrick, Joanne. _The Whole Child_. St. Louis: College Publishing, 1984.

Jampolsky, Gerald G. _Good Bye to Guilt_. Bantam Books, 1985.

Jampolsky, Gerald G. _Love is Letting Go of Fear_. Celestial Arts, 1979.

Jampolsky, Gerald G. _Teach Only Love_. Bantam Books, 1983.

Moorman, Chick. _Talk Sense to Yourself: The Language of Personal Power_. Personal Power Press, 1985.

Progrebin, Letty Cottin. _Growing Up Free_. Bantam Books, 1981.

Pollard, John K. _Self Parenting_. Generic Human Studies Publishing, 1987.

Rimm, Sylvia B. _Underachievement Syndrome_. Apple Publishing Company, 1986.

Seldman, Martin L. _Performance Without Pressure_. Walker and Company, 1988.

Unell, Barbara C., and Wyckoff, Jerry. _Discipline Without Shouting Or Spanking_. Meadowbrook Inc., 1984.

Vygotsky, Lev Semenovich. _Thought and Language_. The M.I.T. Press, 1981.

TRAININGS AND WORKSHOPS

Professional training on the concepts presented in this book is available through the following sources:

CHICK MOORMAN

INSTITUTE FOR PERSONAL POWER
P.O. Box 5985
Saginaw, MI 48603
517-791-3533

NANCY MOORMAN / WEBER

NANCY SPEAKING ... For & About Kids
P.O. Box 1130
Bay City, MI 48706
517-686-3251

TRAINING OPTIONS INCLUDE:

90- to 120-minute overview of the phrases and concepts presented in this book. Thought-provoking and entertaining.

One half-day seminar covering phrases selected for your particular grade levels or situation. Participants have an opportunity to go in-depth on selected concepts. Interactive, entertaining, and practical.

One-day training involves in-depth exposure to the phrases and concepts in this book. Customized for the particular grade levels and group. Lecture bursts, discussion, small group activities are the delivery system for increasing participants' awareness and skills.

The above trainings are available for parent groups. Ask about: PARENT TALK: WHAT IT REALLY MEANS.